RIBBON
KNITS

RIBBON KNITS

45 new
designs
to knit
and
crochet

ξ

Judi Alweil

The Taunton Press

Book publisher: Jim Childs
Acquisitions editor: Jolynn Gower
Publishing coordinator: Sarah Coe
Editor: Thomas McKenna
Designer/layout artist: Lynne Phillips
Photographer: Jack Deutsch
Illustrator: Rosalie Vaccaro
Typeface: Centaur/GillSans
Printer: R. R. Donnelley, Willard, Ohio

Inspiration for hands-on living™

Printed in the United States of America
10 9 8 7 6 5 4 3 2

The Taunton Press, Inc., 63 South Main Street
P.O. Box 5506, Newtown, CT 06470-5506
e-mail: tp@taunton.com

Distributed by Publishers Group West

Library of Congress Cataloging-in-Publication Data
Alweil, Judi
        Ribbon knits: 45 new designs to knit and crochet / Judi Alweil.
              p.   cm.
        ISBN 1-56158-244-1
        1. Knitting—Patterns. 2. Crocheting—Patterns. 3. Ribbon work. I. Title
        TT820.A53   1998
        746.43'20432—dc21   97-47034
                                                                 CIP

To my mother-in-law, Harriet Alweil, my first partner in needlework

Acknowledgments

Acknowledgments are due to the following people, my support structure during the preparation of this book:

My husband, Dick, for his patience, understanding, and hard work.

Karen Alweil Helfman, the "Co." of Judi & Co., for her enthusiasm and encouragement.

Anne Rubin, for working up several of the bag patterns and for her vast knowledge of knitting and crocheting techniques.

Judy Ahmed, for two of the beautiful Luminesse designs.

Liz Tekus, for her Rococo jacket.

Lawrence Schiff Silk Mills, for contributing much of the woven ribbon used in this book.

Rochelle Weissberg, my former partner in Gemini Innovations, with whom I discovered the enjoyment of working with ribbon many years ago.

Carla Scott, for the wonderful job she did in assuring that all of the instructions are correct.

And, of course, the wonderful people at The Taunton Press, including Jolynn Gower, Sarah Coe, and Tom McKenna.

Contents

Introduction

Ribbon is a woven narrow fabric that can have shine, shimmer, and lots of glimmer. I love working with its silky texture and bright colors. I love to wrap, decorate, embroider, and needlepoint with it. Most of all, I love to knit with ribbon.

Today, ribbon can be made from a variety of fabrics, including rayon, silk, or cotton. Of these, many different types are available for knitting and crocheting. Metallic threads can be woven into the warp or weft of a ribbon. Colors can be solids or hand-dyed multicolors with or without accents, which can be made into contemporary, sophisticated, or traditional knitting patterns. The satisfaction of making a sweater, bag, or accessory with beautiful ribbon and getting professional results in a short period of time inspires many knitters to work with this material.

I have used all kinds of ribbon over the years for different projects with wonderful results. In this book I want to share with you various knitting and crocheting projects that have inspired my love for working with ribbon. Many of the projects have interesting textures and trims, allowing you to create your own wearable art using ribbon with accents of other fibers and trims.

Whether you are a beginner, intermediate, or experienced knitter or crocheter, you will find some project that will inspire you. There are quick-and-easy scarves, bags, and vests for the beginner as well as more complicated sweaters, bags, and accessories that incorporate different stitches and fibers. The sweaters are designated beginner or intermediate while the accessories have no designation. Most of the accessories are fairly easy to knit or crochet with basic stitches. The trick is in the finishing. I've given some hints in my instructions for each item, but you may wish to take advantage of your local yarn shop for expert finishing.

I believe you will enjoy making these projects as much as I have. They are exciting to do and result in a quality item that is beautiful to wear and to use.

Basics

GAUGE

Your gauge will determine the size of the piece being knitted or crocheted. The directions have been figured mathematically, based on the number of stitches per inch. You must knit according to the gauge in the directions, and check as you go along to be sure that it remains the same.

To knit or crochet a gauge, you need to use the same materials, needle or crochet size, and pattern stitch specified in the directions. A 4" by 4" square is a good size. To knit a square of this size with a gauge of 2½ sts = 1", cast on 10 stitches. Make sure to use the size needle specified in the directions. Work the pattern for 4". Take the stitches off the needle and measure the square.

Note that ribbon sweaters have a lot of give, and sizing can be a little more general than garments made out of other yarns. If your gauge is incorrect, go to smaller- or larger-size needles. You can also adjust the size of the garment by changing the needle size.

TYING ON ANOTHER SKEIN

It is best to tie on a new skein of ribbon when you come to the end of a row. If this is not practical, start the new skein before you have finished the old one. Leave approximately 4" of unused yarn on both skeins. Work a few rows before tying the loose ends of yarn together. This way, you can control the tension on the knot. Work the ends into the back side of the work.

Always cut ribbon diagonally to avoid raveling.

FINISHING

Block finished pieces of sweater or article carefully with a Teflon-coated iron or by using a pressing cloth. Set the iron at the coolest wool setting and use a small amount of steam.

Three-needle bind-off

This will give the garment a flatter shoulder seam. (With this method, the shoulders do not get bound off and then sewn together.)

Take stitches off stitch holders and place on smaller needles both facing the same direction. Place right sides (inside out) together. Backstitches are on one needle; front stitches are on the other. Knit two together (one stitch from front needle and one stitch from back needle). Repeat and slip the first stitch off over the second stitch. Continue binding off in this manner across the row until all stitches are bound off.

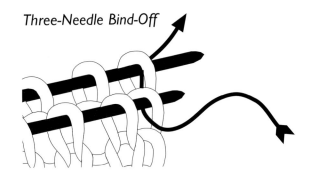

Three-Needle Bind-Off

Sewing Pieces Together

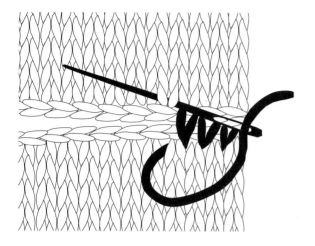

Sewing pieces together

Lay the pieces to be joined vertically side by side, right-side up. Using a tapestry needle threaded with ribbon that matches the garment yarn, insert the needle from the back side into the bottom edge of the work, one row of stitches away from the side edge. When you stretch the knitting slightly, little ladders of yarn appear within and between the rows of stitches. Use these as a guide.

Bring the needle through from the back of the work over the first row of stitches, over the top, and down between the first two rows of stitches of the second piece. Come up through the second piece, catching one "rung" of yarn. Cross over the top and catch a rung of yarn on the other piece. Repeat this by catching every row in turn. Pull the yarn up gently and uniformly every two or three stitches. You will be making a seam on the wrong side, but the right side of the work will not show a seam.

When weaving together horizontal pieces, you will want them to appear seamless. Lay the pieces right-side up, butting the edges to be joined. The knit stitches are a succession of little Vs, which must appear to be knitted together. Bring the needle from behind the work, starting as near the edge of the work as possible, from the center of the first open V. Bring the needle over the top and pick up both pieces of yarn that meet at the bottom of the V of the stitch above. Bring the needle back over the top and into the center of the open V from which you started. Pick up the tip of the inverted V of the next stitch. Bring the needle up, across the seam, and into the open end of the stitch above.

Continue across the row in this way, pulling the yarn gently every two or three stitches and being careful to maintain even tension.

Whipstitching

This is an overcast stitch that is simple to do.

Crochet Insert the needle at a right angle under the back loop of a corresponding stitch on each edge. Draw the yarn through.

Knit Insert the needle at a right angle under one stitch on one piece, then under one strand of a corresponding stitch on the other piece. Pull the yarn through.

Crochet Whipstitch

Knit Whipstitch

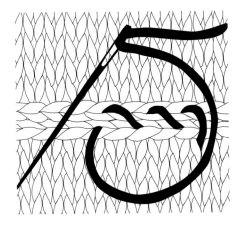

HOW TO COVER A RING

Insert the hook into the center of the ring and pull a loop of ribbon (or yarn) back through the ring. Place both ends of ribbon over the hook and pull them through the loop on the hook. Use the double ribbon only for the first stitch. Work in single crochet around the entire ring until it's covered. Join with a slip-stitch to the first stitch. Fasten off.

How to Cover a Ring

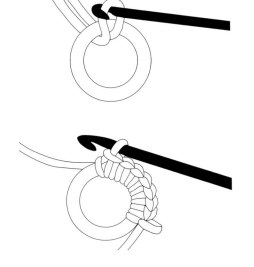

CARE OF FINISHED GARMENTS

Rayon ribbon has a silky appearance and dyes beautifully. The sweaters can be worn in all seasons but require care. You have created beautiful wearable art, and it should be treated as such. Dry cleaning by a reliable dry cleaner is recommended. *Do not wash rayon.* Most of these sweaters are knit rather loosely and will stretch if not folded. Never hang the sweater as it will stretch in the length, and the hanger will distort the shoulders.

ALTERNATING SKEINS

When working with hand-dyed ribbons, it is advisable to alternate skeins (work two rows from one ball and two rows from the next ball) to avoid a difference in colors, even if yarn or ribbon is all from the same dye lot. Some skeins may get more color than others in the dyeing process.

LINING

Lining is suggested on some bags, but it's required for the Patchwork Drawstring Bag on p. 94. You can attempt this yourself or enlist the help of a dressmaker or upholsterer.

To line a bag, trace the shape of the bag for your lining pattern. Cut two pieces of lining. Sew them together and, without turning inside out, put the lining in the bag. Fold under the top of the lining ½" to ⅝" to hide the raw edge, and slipstitch to the top of the bag.

Knitting Abbreviations

approx	approximately	pat(s)	pattern(s)	SSK	slip, slip, knit: Slip next 2 sts knitwise, one at a time, to RH needle. Insert LH needle into fronts of sts from left to right and k sts tog.
beg	begin(ning)	pat st	pattern stitch		
CC	contrasting color	psso	pass slipped stitches over		
cn	cable needle				
cont	continue	RH	right hand		
dec	decrease(s)(d)(ing)	rem	remaining	St st	Stockinette stitch
dp	double pointed	rep	repeat	st(s)	stitch(es)
"	inch(es)	rev	reverse	tbl	through back of loop(s)
inc	increase(s)(d)(ing)	rev St st	reverse Stockinette stitch		
k	knit			tog	together
LH	left hand	rnd	round	WS	wrong side
MC	main color	RS	right side	wyb	with yarn back
P	purl	SKP	slip 1, knit 1, psso	wyf	with yarn forward
		sl	slip	yd(s)	yard(s)
				Yo	yarn over needle

NOTES
- Stitches that follow a star * in a pattern row must be repeated from that point.
- Stitch combinations enclosed in square brackets [ ] must be repeated in the order shown.

Crocheting Abbreviations

approx	approximately	lp(s)	loop(s)	sk	skip
beg	begin(ning)	MC	main color	sl st	slipstitch
CC	contrasting color	pat(s)	pattern(s)	sp	space
ch	chain	rem	remaining	st(s)	stitch(es)
cont	continue	rep	repeat	tog	together
dc	double crochet	rev	reverse	tr	triple or treble crochet
dec	decrease(s)(d)(ing)	RH	right hand		
hdc	half double crochet	rnd(s)	round(s)	WS	wrong side
"	inch(es)	RS	right side	yd(s)	yard(s)
inc	increase(s)(d)(ing)	sc	single crochet	Yo	yarn over
LH	left hand				

NOTES
- Stitches that follow a star * in a pattern row must be repeated from that point.
- Stitch combinations enclosed in square brackets [ ] must be repeated in the order shown.
- A slipstitch in crochet directions is a *non*-stitch and does not count as a stitch.

Chapter 1

SWEATERS

W hether you are planning an outfit for a special occasion or a casual and comfortable top to wear with jeans, you will find a sweater in this chapter to appeal to your creative instincts. There are plenty of seasonless, quick-to-knit cropped tops and tunic sweaters, some with sleeves, some without.

Random Stripes

This sweater would look equally well in hand-dyed ½" ribbon or a solid color with embellishments on the shoulder. Instructions follow for a tunic-length top and a cropped top.

Level of experience Beginner

Sizes Small (medium, large, extra-large) Instructions are for size small. Changes for sizes medium, large, and extra-large are in parentheses.

Finished measurements
Bust at underarm 38 (41, 43, 46)"
Length Tunic: 20 (20½, 21, 21½)"
Cropped top: 15 (16, 17, 17½)"

Gauge In St st, 10 sts and 14 rows = 4" using size 15 needles.

MATERIALS

- Judi & Co.'s ½" ribbon (100% rayon, 100-yd spool), 4 (5, 5, 6) spools assorted colors (Mauve, Winter Plum, Crystal, Powder Blue). For solid colors: tunic: 4 (5, 5, 6) spools; cropped vest: 3 (4, 4, 5) spools
- Straight knitting needles size 15, or size to obtain gauge
- Yarn needle
- Crochet hook size I/9

Pat st Garter st: K every row.
Stripes are done at random. The choice is up to you. Front and back do not have to match. Stripes can even be broken in the middle of a row and new color attached. Ends can be brought to right side, knotted tog, and left hanging about 2".

BACK

Cast on 48 (51, 54, 57) sts. Work in garter st until tunic measures 13 (13, 13, 13½)" and vest measures 8 (8½, 9, 9½)".

SHAPE ARMHOLE

Bind off 5 sts at beg of next 2 rows: 38 (41, 44, 47) sts. Work even until armhole measures 7 (7½, 8, 8)". Bind off all sts loosely.

FRONT

Work same as back.

FINISHING

Block pieces to measurements. Sew side seams, leaving 5" (tunic) or 2½" (top) open at lower edge for slits. Sew shoulder seams, leaving large enough opening for head.

OPTIONAL

With RS facing and crochet hook, work 1 row sc around armhole and neck edge in any color.
Or cut four strips of leftover ribbon and make a bow for one shoulder. Put a large hole bead on each ribbon end. Tie a knot to prevent bead from slipping off. (This would look best on the hand-dyed or solid color sweater.)

Tunic version

15 (16½, 17½, 18½)"

7 (7½, 8, 8)"

20 (20½, 21, 21½)"

19 (20½, 21½, 23)"

Cropped version

15 (16½, 17½, 18½)"

7 (7½, 8, 8)"

15 (16, 17, 17½)"

19 (20½, 21½, 23)"

Sleeveless V-Neck Lace Pullover

Level of experience Intermediate

Sizes Small (medium, large)
Instructions are for size small. Changes for sizes medium and large are in parentheses.

Finished measurements
Bust at underarm 34 (37, 40)"
Length 19 (20½, 22)"

Gauge In lace pat, 11 sts and 14 rows = 4" using size 11 needles.

LACE PAT (multiple of 10 sts plus 1)

Rows 1 and 3 (WS) P.
Row 2 K1, *yo, k3, sl 1—k2 tog—psso, k3, yo k1; rep from *.
Row 4 P1, *k1, yo, k2, sl 1—k2 tog—psso, k2, yo, k1, p1; rep from *.
Rows 5 and 7 K1, *p9, k1; rep from *.
Row 6 P1, *k2, yo, k1, sl 1—k2 tog—psso, k1, yo, k2, p1; rep from *.
Row 8 P1, *k3, yo, sl 1—k2 tog—psso, yo, k3, p1; rep from *.
Rep rows 1-8 for lace pat.

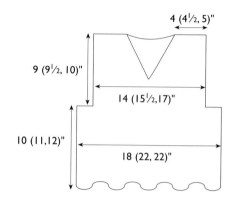

MATERIALS

- Judi & Co.'s Luminesse (100% rayon, 100 yds each), 3 (4, 4) skeins Japanese Maple
- Straight knitting needles size 11, or size to obtain gauge
- Crochet hook size H (optional)

BACK

With size 11 needles, cast on 51 (61, 61) sts. Work 32 rows in lace pat. P next row on WS, dec 4 (10, 6) sts evenly across—47 (51, 55) sts. Work in St st (k on RS, p on WS) until piece measures 10 (11, 12)" from bottom of scallop.

SHAPE ARMHOLE

Bind off 4 sts beg of next 2 rows—39 (43, 47) sts. Work 4 sts each end in garter st (k every row) for length of armhole. Work even until armhole measures 8½ (9, 9½)".

SHAPE NECK

Work 12 (14, 16) sts, join second ball of ribbon, bind off center 15 sts, work to end. Working both sides at once, dec 1 st at each neck edge every other row once—11 (13, 15) sts. Bind off or put on stitch holders for three-needle bind-off.

FRONT

Work same as back until armhole measures 2½". End with a WS row.

SHAPE V-NECK

Work 19 (21, 23) sts, join second ball and k2 tog, work to end. Working both sides at the same time, work 1 row even.

Next row (RS) Work to last 3 sts, k2 tog, k1; on second half, k1, SSK, work to end of row. Work 1 row even. Rep last 2 rows until 11 (13, 15) sts rem. Work even until same length as back. Bind off or put on stitch holders for three-needle bind-off.

FINISHING

Block pieces to measurements. Follow instructions for three-needle bind-off or sew shoulder seams. Sew side seams.

OPTIONAL

With RS facing and crochet hook, work 1 row sc around neck edge.

Side-to-Side Ribbon Sweater

Level of experience Intermediate

Sizes Small (medium, large)
Instructions are for size small. Changes for sizes medium and large are in parentheses.

Finished measurements
Bust at underarm 44 (46, 48)"
Length 20¾ (22½, 23¾)"

Gauge In pat I, 10 sts and 16 rows = 4" using size 11 needles.

Notes When changing colors, carry yarn not in use alongside of work to avoid weaving in many ends.
This sweater is knitted side to side. Back and front are knit separately.

PAT I (8 rows)

With C, p2 rows. With B, p2 rows. With A, work in St st for 2 rows. With B, work in St st for 2 rows.

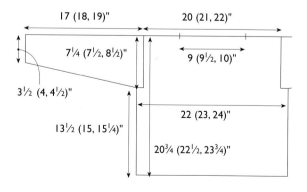

17 (18, 19)" 20 (21, 22)"

7¼ (7½, 8½)" 9 (9½, 10)"

3½ (4, 4½)"

13½ (15, 15¼)" 22 (23, 24)"

20¾ (22½, 23¾)"

MATERIALS

- Judi & Co.'s ½" Rayon Knitting Ribbon (100% rayon, 100 yds each), 2 (3, 4) spools Ecru (A)
- Judi & Co.'s ¼" Rayon Knitting Ribbon (100% rayon, 100 yds each), 2 (3, 4) spools Ecru (B)
- Judi & Co.'s Petite Satin Cord (70 yds each), 3 (4, 4) spools Putty (C)
- Straight knitting needles size 11
- Crochet hook size H

PAT II (12 rows)

With C, p2 rows. With B, p2 rows. [With A, work in St st for 2 rows. With B, work in St st for 2 rows] twice.

BACK

With B, cast on 34 (36, 38) sts. P next row on WS. Join A and work in St st for 2 rows. With B, work in St st for 2 rows. With B, cast on 18 (20, 22) sts for armhole at beg of next RS row—52 (56, 60) sts. Work pat I once. Work pat II once. Work pat I twice. Work pat II once, then rep last 4 rows of pat II 0 (1, 2) times more. Work pat I twice. Work pat II once. Work pat I once. Work first 4 rows of pat I once. Change to B and bind off 18 (20, 22) sts at beg of next RS row for armhole, p to end—34 (36, 38) sts. P next row. With A, work in St st for 2 rows. With B, work in St st for 2 rows. Bind off all sts.

FRONT

Work same as back.

SLEEVES

With B, cast on 20 (24, 28) sts. P next row on WS.
Work last 4 rows of pat II, then pat II once, pat I
twice, pat II once, pat I three times. Rep last 4
rows of Pat I to end of sleeve, *at the same time*, inc
1 st each side every fourth row 10 (12, 14) times
from beg of sleeves—40 (48, 56) sts. Work even
until piece measures 17 (18, 19)" from beg, or
length desired. Bind off all sts loosely.

FINISHING

Sew shoulder seams, leaving center 9½ (10, 10½)"
unsewn for neck opening. Set in sleeves. Sew
side and sleeve seams. Weave in all ends.
With RS facing, crochet hook and A, work 1
row sc around lower edge of sweater and neck
opening. With B, work 1 row sc around lower
edge of sleeves.

Cropped T-Shirt

Level of experience Beginner

Sizes Petite (small, medium, large)
Instructions are for size petite. Changes
for sizes small, medium, and large are in
parentheses.

Finished measurements
Bust at underarm 38 (40, 42, 44)"
Length 18 (19, 19½, 20½)"

Gauge In rev St st, 10 sts and 14 rows = 4"
using size 15 needles.

Note This sweater also looks great on St st
side.

BACK

With larger needles, cast on 40 (42, 44, 47) sts.
Work in rev St st (p on RS, k on WS), inc 1 st
each side every 1" 4 times—48 (50, 52, 55) sts.
Work even until piece measures 9 (9½, 9½, 10)"
from beg.

SHAPE ARMHOLES

Bind off 4 sts at beg of next 2 rows. Dec 1 st each
side every other row twice—36 (38, 40, 43) sts.

MATERIALS

- Judi & Co. ½" Rayon Knitting Ribbon
  (100% rayon, 100-yd spool), 3 (4, 5, 6)
  spools
- Straight knitting needles sizes 10 and 15,
  or sizes to obtain gauge
- Crochet hook size H

Work even until armhole measures 7½ (8, 8½, 9)".

SHAPE SHOULDERS AND NECK

Bind off 3 (3, 3, 4) sts at beg of next 4 (2, 2, 6)
rows, 4 sts at beg of next 2 (4, 4, 0) rows. *At the
same time*, after 2 rows of shoulder shaping have
been worked, bind off center 16 (16, 18, 19) sts
for neck and work both sides with separate
spools of ribbon.

FRONT

Work same as back until armhole measures
3½ (4, 4½, 5)".

SHAPE NECK

Work 14 (15, 15, 16) sts, bind off center 8 (8, 10,
11) sts for neck, work to end. Working both sides
with separate spools of ribbon, dec 1 st at each
neck edge every other row 4 times, *at the same
time*, when same length as back to shoulder, shape
shoulders as on back.

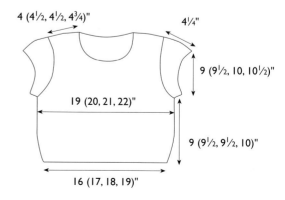

SHAPE SLEEVES

With smaller needles, cast on 34 (36, 38, 40) sts.
Change to larger needles and work in rev St st,
inc 1 st each side every other row twice—38 (40,
42, 44) sts. Work even until piece measures 2"
from beg.

SHAPE CAP

Bind off 4 sts at beg of next 8 rows. Bind off rem
6 (8, 10, 12) sts.

FINISHING

Block pieces to measurements. Sew shoulder
seams. Set in sleeves. Sew side seams and sleeve
seams. With RS facing and crochet hook, work sl
st loosely around neck edge.

Scattered Stripes

Level of experience Beginner

Sizes Petite (small, medium, large)
Instructions are for size petite. Changes for sizes small, medium, and large are in parentheses.

Finished measurements
Bust at underarm 38 (41, 43, 46)"
Length 18½ (19½, 20½, 21½)"

Gauge In St st, 10 sts and 14 rows = 4" using size 13 needles.

Note All stripes in CC are worked in garter st (k every row).

BACK

With MC, cast on 48 (51, 54, 57) sts and work in k2, p2 rib for ½", end with a WS row. Work 4 rows in St st.
*Next row (RS) With MC, k27 (29, 31, 33), join CC and k21 (22, 23, 24) sts.
Next row (WS) With CC, k21 (22, 23, 24), with MC, p27 (29, 31, 33). Be careful to twist yarn when changing color to prevent holes. Cont in St st with MC only for 8 rows.
Next row (RS) With CC, k21 (22, 23, 24), with MC, k27 (29, 31, 33).
Next row (WS) With MC, p27 (29, 31,33), with CC, k21 (22, 23, 24). Cont in St st with MC only for 8 rows. Rep from * (20 rows) for stripe pat until piece measures 10½ (11, 12, 12½)" from beg. End with a WS row.

MATERIALS

- Judi & Co.'s ½" Rayon Knitting Ribbon (100% rayon, 100-yd spool), 4 (4, 5, 6) spools Pale Pink (MC)
- 1 spool Black (CC)
- Straight knitting needles size 15, or size to obtain gauge
- Crochet hook size H

SHAPE SLEEVES

Cast on 2 sts at beg of next 2 rows, 3 sts at beg of next 2 rows—58 (61, 64, 67) sts. Cont in stripe pat until armhole measures 7½ (8, 8½, 9)".

SHAPE NECK

Work 22 (23, 24, 25) sts, join second spool of MC and bind off center 14 (15, 16, 17) sts for neck, work to end. Working both sides at the same time with separate spools, dec 1 st at each neck edge on next RS row. When sleeve measures 8 (8½, 9, 9½)", bind off or put 21 (22, 23, 24) sts each side on holders.

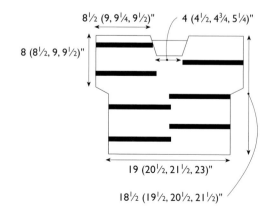

8½ (9, 9¼, 9½)"   4 (4½, 4¾, 5¼)"

8 (8½, 9, 9½)"

19 (20½, 21½, 23)"

18½ (19½, 20½, 21½)"

FRONT

Work as for back until piece measures 15 (15½, 16, 16½)" from beg.

SHAPE NECK

Work 24 (25, 26, 27) sts, join second spool of ribbon, bind off center 10 (11, 12, 13) sts for neck, work to end. Working both sides at the same time with separate spools, dec 1 st at each neck edge every RS row 3 times. Work even until same length as back. Bind off or put 21 (22, 23, 24) sts each side on holders.

FINISHING

Block pieces to measurements. Sew shoulder seams or follow instructions for knitting shoulder seams tog. Sew side seams and weave in all ends. With RS facing, crochet hook, and MC, work 1 row sc around neck and sleeves.

Reversible Color Block Sweater

Level of experience Intermediate

Sizes Small (medium, large)
Instructions are for size small. Changes for sizes medium and large are in parentheses.

Finished measurements
Bust at underarm 42 (45, 48)"
Length 17 (18, 19)"

Gauge In St st, 10 sts and 14 rows = 4" using size 15 needles.

BACK

With A, cast on 26 (28, 30) sts, join MC, and cast on 26 (28, 30) sts, for a total of 52 (56, 60) sts. P1 row on WS, matching colors. Change to St st and work until piece measures 7 (7½, 8)" from beg. Make sure to twist the ribbon on WS to prevent holes when changing colors.

SHAPE ARMHOLE

Bind off 3 sts at beg of next 2 rows, 2 sts at beg of next 2 rows—42 (46, 50) sts. Work even until piece measures 14½ (15, 16)" from beg.

MATERIALS

- Judi & Co's ½" Rayon Knitting Ribbon (100% rayon, 100-yd spool), 2 spools Blue (MC), 1 (1, 2) spools each Olive (A) and Copper (B), 1 spool Black (C)
- Straight knitting needles size 15, or size to obtain gauge
- Crochet hook size H

SHAPE NECK

Work 13 (14, 16) sts, join a new length of same color ribbon, and bind off center 16 (18, 18) sts, making sure to change colors in the center of bind-off, work to end. Working both sides at the same time with separate ribbon, dec 1 st at each neck edge on next RS row. Work even on rem 12 (13, 14) sts for each shoulder until armhole measures 10 (10½, 11)". Bind off or put shoulder sts on holders for three-needle bind-off.

FRONT

With B, cast on 26 (28, 30) sts, with MC, cast on 26 (28, 30) sts, for a total of 52 (56, 60) sts. Complete same as back.

FINISHING

Block pieces to measurements. Sew shoulder and side seams.

TRIM

With RS facing, crochet hook, and C, work sc around armholes, neck (work 3 sc in each corner of neck), and lower edge of sweater. Work 1 row of sc down center of sweater on top of color change.
With C, work duplicate st heart following graph (see the photo on the facing page for placement).

OPTIONAL

Several more hearts may be placed on sweater in random places.

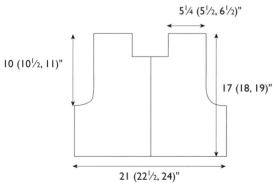

5¼ (5½, 6½)"

10 (10½, 11)"

17 (18, 19)"

21 (22½, 24)"

Stitch pattern for hearts

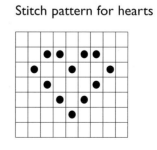

Fitted Cropped Sweater

Level of experience Intermediate

Sizes Small (medium, large)
Instructions are for size small. Changes for
sizes medium and large are in parentheses.

Finished measurements
Bust at underarm 36 (38, 40½)"
Length 15½ (16, 16½)"

Gauges
In k1, p2 rib, 16 sts and 18 rows = 4" using
smaller needles. In k1, p5 rib, 14 sts and 16
rows = 4" using larger needles.

K1, P2 RIB

Row 1 (RS) *K1, p2; rep from * to end.
Row 2 K the knit sts and p the purl sts.
Rep rows 1 and 2 for k1, p2 rib.

K1, P5 RIB

Row 1 (RS) *K1, p5; rep from * to end.
Row 2 K the knit sts and p the purl sts.
Rep rows 1 and 2 for k1, p5 rib.

MATERIALS

- Judi & Co.'s Putty Charmeuse (70 yds each), 3 (4, 4) spools (A)
- Judi & Co.'s ¼" (Cement) Ribbon (100 yds each), 3 (3, 4) spools (B)
- Straight knitting needles sizes 10½ and 11, or sizes to obtain gauge
- Circular knitting needle size 9

STRIPE PAT

Work *10 rows B, 3 rows A*. Rep between *s (13
rows) for stripe pat.

BACK

With smaller straight needles and A, cast on 53
(57, 61) sts.
Beg k1, p2 rib—Row 1 (RS) P2 (1, 0), [k1, p2]
17 (18, 20) times, k0 (1, 1), p0 (1, 0). Cont in rib as
established, inc 1 st each end (working inc sts into
rib) every 1½" twice—57 (61, 65) sts. Work even
until piece measures 3¾" from beg. Change to
larger needles and B.
Beg k1, p5 rib—Row 1 (RS) P4 (3, 5), [k1, p5] 8
(10, 11) times, k1 (1, 0), p4 (3, 0). Cont in rib as
established, *and* working in stripe pat, inc 1 st each
end (working inc sts into rib), every ¾" 3 times—
63 (67, 71) sts. Work even until piece measures
7½" from beg.

SHAPE ARMHOLE

Bind off 5 sts at beg of next 2 rows, dec 1 st each
end every other row 4 (4, 5) times—45 (49, 51)
sts. Work even until piece measures 14½ (15,
15½)" from beg.

SHAPE NECK

Next row (RS) Work 11 (13, 14) sts, slip next 23
sts to a holder, join second ball of yarn, work rem
11 (13, 14) sts. Working both sides at the same
time, dec 1 st at each neck edge on next RS row.
Work even until piece measures 15½ (16, 16½)"
from beg. Bind off or put on stitch holder for
three-needle bind-off.

FRONT

Work same as back until piece measures 12½ (13,
13½)" from beg.

Fitted Cropped Sweater

Back and front

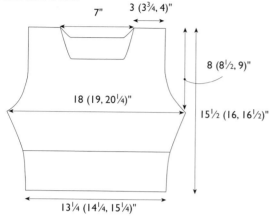

Sleeve

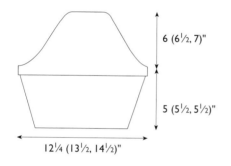

SHAPE NECK

Next row (RS) Work 15 (17, 18) sts, slip next 15 sts to a holder, join second ball of yarn, work rem 15 (17, 18) sts. Working both sides at once, bind off from each neck edge 2 sts once, dec 1 st every other row twice—11 (13, 14) sts each side. Work even until piece measures same as back. Bind off or put on stitch holder for three-needle bind-off.

SLEEVES

With smaller, straight needles and A, cast on 35 (39, 43) sts.
Beg k1, p2 rib—Row 1 (RS) P2 (1, 0), [k1, p2] 11 (12, 14) times, k0 (1, 1), p0 (1, 0). Cont in rib as established, inc 1 st each end (working inc sts into rib) every fourth row 4 times—43 (47, 51) sts. Change to larger needles and B.
Beg k1, p5 rib—Row 1 (RS) P3 (5, 4), [k1, p5] 6 (6, 7) times, k1, p3 (5, 4). Cont in rib as established, *and* working in stripe pat, until piece measures 5 (5½, 5½)" from beg.

SHAPE CAP

Bind off 5 sts at beg of next 2 rows, 2 sts at beg of next 2 rows. Dec 1 st each end every other row 8 (11, 12) times, every fourth row 1 (0, 0) times. Bind off rem 11 (11, 13) sts.

FINISHING

Block pieces to measurements. Sew shoulder seams. Set in sleeves. Sew side and sleeve seams.

NECKBAND

With RS facing, circular needle, and A, pick up 66 sts evenly around neck edge, including sts on holders. Join and work k1, p2 rib for 4 rnds. Bind off loosely.

Double-Breasted Ribbon Jacket and Shell

Double-breasted ribbon jacket

Level of experience Intermediate

Sizes Small (medium, large)
Instructions are for size small. Changes for sizes medium and large are in parentheses.

Finished measurements
Bust at underarm 38 (40, 42)"
Length 21 (22, 23)"

Gauge In St st, 14 sts and 20 rows = 4" using size 10½ needle.

BACK

With 10½ needles, cast on 60 (64, 68) sts. Work in St st (k on RS, p on WS), inc 1 st each end every sixteenth row 3 times—66 (70, 74) sts. Work even until piece measures 13 (13½, 14)" from beg.

MATERIALS

- **For jacket** Judi & Co.'s ¼" Rayon Knitting Ribbon (100% rayon, 100 yds each), 10 (11, 12) spools
- **For shell** Judi & Co.'s ¼" Rayon Knitting Ribbon (100% rayon, 100 yds), 5 (6, 6, 7) spools
- Straight knitting needles size 10½, or size to obtain gauge
- Crochet hook size F
- Yarn needle
- Four 1" (approx) diameter buttons

SHAPE ARMHOLE

Bind off 4 (4, 5) sts at beg of next 2 rows, dec 1 st each end every other row 3 (4, 4) times—52 (54, 56) sts. Work even until armhole measures 7¼ (7¾, 8¼)".

SHAPE NECK

Next row Work 21 (22, 23) sts, join second spool of ribbon, and bind off center 10 sts, work to end. Working both sides at the same time, bind off from each neck edge 4 sts once. Work even until armhole measures 8 (8½, 9)". Bind off rem 17 (18, 19) sts each side for shoulders.

RIGHT FRONT

For pocket lining, cast on 14 sts and work 20 rows in St st. Sl sts to holders.
Cast on 41 (43, 45) sts. Work in St st, working incs and armhole shaping at side edge (end of RS rows) same as back, *at the same time*, when pieces measure 1¼" from beg, work buttonholes at front edge: At beg of a RS row, work 2 sts, bind off 2 sts, work 15 sts, bind off 2 sts, work to end. Next row, cast on 2 sts over each set of bound-off sts. When piece measures 5½" from beg, work second set of buttonholes as before. When piece measures 6 (6½, 7)" from beg, shape neck.

SHAPE NECK

Dec 1 st at neck edge (beg of RS rows) every other row 5 (4, 3) times, then every fourth row 15 (16, 17) times, *at the same time*, when piece measures 12½ (13, 13½)" from beg, on RS, make pocket.

MAKE POCKET

Work 4 sts, bind off next 14 sts for pocket opening, work to end. On next row, p to pocket

Double-Breasted Ribbon Jacket

Back

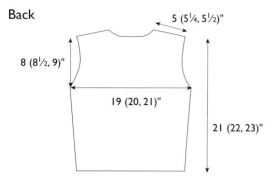

5 (5¼, 5½)"

8 (8½, 9)"

19 (20, 21)"

21 (22, 23)"

Right front

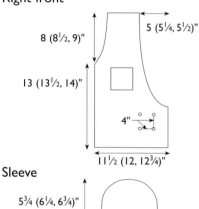

5 (5¼, 5½)"

8 (8½, 9)"

13 (13½, 14)"

4"

11½ (12, 12¾)"

Sleeve

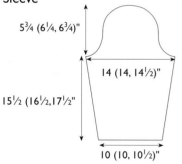

5¾ (6¼, 6¾)"

14 (14, 14½)"

15½ (16½, 17½)"

10 (10, 10½)"

Shell

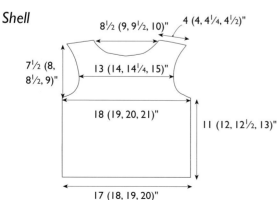

8½ (9, 9½, 10)"   4 (4, 4¼, 4½)"

7½ (8, 8½, 9)"

13 (14, 14¼, 15)"

18 (19, 20, 21)"

11 (12, 12½, 13)"

17 (18, 19, 20)"

opening, p lining sts from holder, p to end. When piece measures 13 (13½, 14)" from beg, shape armhole at side edge same as on back. After all neck decs have been worked, work even on rem 17 (18, 19) sts until same length as back. Bind off.

LEFT FRONT

Work to correspond to right front, reversing shaping and omitting buttonholes and pocket.

SHAPE SLEEVES

Cast on 35 (35, 37) sts. Work in St st, inc 1 st each end every eighth row 3 times, then every tenth row 4 times—49 (49, 51) sts. Work even until piece measures 15½ (16½, 17½)" from beg, or desired length.

SHAPE CAP

Bind off 3 sts at beg of next 2 rows, 2 sts at beg of next 2 rows, dec 1 st each end every other row 9 (7, 8) times, every fourth row 1 (3, 3) times. Bind off 2 sts at beg of next 2 rows. Bind off rem 15 sts.

FINISHING

Block pieces to measurements. Sew shoulder seams. Set in sleeves. Sew side and sleeve seams. Sew pocket lining in place to WS of front. With RS facing and crochet hook, work 2 rnds sc around outside edge of jacket, sleeve edges, and top of pocket. Sew on buttons.

Shell

Level of experience Beginner

Sizes Petite (small, medium, large) Instructions are for size petite. Changes for sizes small, medium, and large are in parentheses.

Finished measurements
Bust at underarm 36 (38, 40, 42)"
Length 18½ (20, 21, 22)"

Gauge In St st, 14 sts and 18 rows = 4"
using size 10½ needle.

BACK

With size 10½ needles, cast on 59 (63, 66, 70)
sts. Work in St st (k on RS, p on WS), inc 1 st
each end every 4", twice—63 (67, 70, 74) sts.
Work even until piece measures 11 (12, 12½, 13)"
from beg.

SHAPE ARMHOLE

Bind off 3 sts at beg of next 4 rows, 2 sts at beg
of next 2 rows, and 1 st at beg of next 2 (2, 4, 6)
rows—45 (49, 50, 52) sts. Work 4 (4, 2, 0) rows
even. Then inc 1 st each end every other row 4

(5, 6, 7) times, at the same time, when piece measures 15½ (17, 18, 19)" from beg, work as follows:

SHAPE NECK

Bind off center 5 (7, 8, 10) sts and, working both
sides at once, bind off from each neck edge 4 sts
once, 3 sts once, 2 sts twice, 1 st once—12 (14,
15, 16) sts each side for shoulders. Work even
until piece measures 18½ (20, 21, 22)" from beg.
Bind off or put on stitch holders for three-needle
bind-off.

FRONT

Work same as back.

FINISHING

Block pieces to measurements. Sew shoulder
and side seams. With RS facing and crochet
hook, work 2 rows sc around neck, armholes, and
lower edges.

Openwork Vest

Level of experience Intermediate

Sizes Small (medium, large)
Instructions are for size small. Changes for sizes medium and large are in parentheses.

Finished measurements
Bust at underarm 39 (42, 45)"
Length 16½ (17½, 18½)"

Gauge In mesh pat, 10 sts and 16 rows = 4" using smaller needles.

MESH PATTERN (over odd number of sts)

Row 1 (RS) K2, *yo, k2 tog; rep from * to last st, end k1.
Rows 2 and 4 P.
Row 3 K1 *SSK, yo; rep from * to last 2 sts, end k2.
Rep rows 1 to 4 for mesh pat.

BACK

With larger needles, cast on 49 (53, 57) sts. Work 2 rows in garter st (k every row).
Change to smaller needles and work in mesh pat until piece measures 8 (8½, 9)" from beg, end with a WS row.

SHAPE ARMHOLE

Change to larger needles and garter st. Bind off 5 sts at beg of next 2 rows—39 (43, 47) sts. Work 2 more rows in garter st. Change to smaller needles and work as follows: K2, place marker, work mesh pat to last 2 sts, place marker, k2. Keeping first and last 2 sts in garter st, work rem sts in mesh pat until armhole measures 8 (8½, 9)". Change to garter st. Do not change needles.

Bind off 11 (12, 14) sts at beg of next 2 rows. Bind off rem 17 (19, 19) sts for back neck.

LEFT FRONT

With larger needles, cast on 29 (31, 33) sts. Work 2 rows in garter st. Change to smaller needles and work in mesh pat, keeping 2 sts at front edge in garter st for entire piece. Work until same length as back to armhole.

SHAPE ARMHOLE

Next row (RS) Bind off 5 sts, k to end. K1 row.
Next row K2, k2 tog, k to end—23 (25, 27) sts. K1 row more. Change to smaller needles and work in mesh pat, keeping first 2 and last 2 sts in garter st, until armhole measures 7 (7½, 8)", end with a RS row.

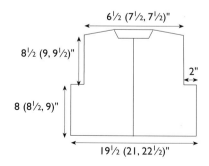

6½ (7½, 7½)"
8½ (9, 9½)"
2"
8 (8½, 9)"
19½ (21, 22½)"

SHAPE NECK

Next row (WS) Bind off 3 sts (neck edge), work to end. Change to larger needles and garter st. Cont to bind off from neck edge 6 (7, 7) sts once, 3 sts once. Work even in garter st until same length as back. Bind off rem 11 (12, 14) sts for shoulder.

RIGHT FRONT

Work to correspond to left front, reversing all shaping.

FINISHING

Block pieces to measurements. Sew shoulder and side seams. Sew button at top of left front just below neck shaping. Eyelet in mesh pat serves as a buttonhole.

Rococo Jacket

Level of experience Beginner

Sizes Petite (small, medium, large)
Instructions are for size petite. Changes
for sizes small, medium, and large are in
parentheses.

Finished measurements
Bust at underarm 33 (35, 37, 39)"
Length 17 (18, 19, 20)"

Gauge In seed st, 8 sts and 11 rows = 4"
using size 11 needles.

SEED ST

Row 1 (RS) *K1, p1; rep from * to end.
Row 2 K the purl sts and p the knit sts.
Rep row 2 for seed st.

BACK

With size 11 needles, cast on 33 (35, 37, 39) sts.
Work in k1, p1 rib for 1". Work in seed st until
piece measures 7 (7½, 8, 8½)" from beg.

SHAPE ARMHOLE

Bind off 3 sts at beg of next 2 rows, 1 st at beg of
next 2 rows—25 (27, 29, 31) sts. Work even until
piece measures 17 (18, 19, 20)" from beg. Bind off
all sts.

MATERIALS

- Judi & Co.'s Rococo (100% rayon, 144
  yds each), 2 (2, 3, 4) spools
- Straight knitting needles size 11, or size
  to obtain gauge
- Three 1" diameter buttons

Body

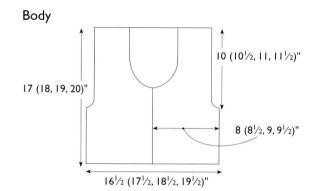

Sleeve

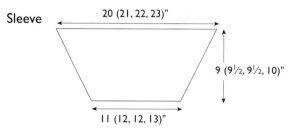

LEFT FRONT

With size 11 needles, cast on 16 (17, 18, 19) sts.
Work as for back until piece measures 7½ (8, 8½,
9)" from beg.

SHAPE ARMHOLE AND NECK

Work armhole shaping at side edge (beg of RS
rows) as for back, *at the same time*, dec 1 st at
neck edge (end of RS rows) on next row, then
every fourth row 5 (5, 6, 6) times more. When
same length as back, bind off rem 6 (7, 7, 8) sts for
shoulder.

RIGHT FRONT

Work as for left front, reversing shaping.

SHAPE SLEEVES

With size 11 needles, cast on 22 (24, 24, 26) sts.
Work in k1, p1 rib for 3 rows. Change to seed st,

inc 1 st each end (working inc sts into seed st) every other row 9 (9, 10, 10) times—40 (42, 44, 46) sts. Work even until piece measures 9 (9½, 9½, 10)" from beg. Bind off 1 st at beg of next 2 rows. Bind off rem sts loosely.

FINISHING

From outside, sew shoulder seams. Center sleeve between armhole edges, placing sleeve straight into armhole. (Do not curve sleeve.) From outside, sew in sleeves. Sew side and sleeve seams from inside using whipstitch.

OUTSIDE EDGING

With RS facing, size 11 needles, beg at lower right front edge, pick up and k16 (17, 18, 19) sts along right front to beg of V shaping, 17 (18, 19, 20) sts to shoulder seam, 13 (13, 15, 15) sts along back neck, work left front to correspond to right front—79 (83, 89, 93) sts.
Next (buttonhole) row (WS) Beg with p1, work in k1, p1 rib to last 16 (17, 18, 19) sts, [yo, k2 tog, rib 4 (4, 5, 5)] twice, yo, k2 tog, rib to end. Work 1 row even in rib. Bind off loosely in rib. Sew on buttons.

Bubble Stitch Tunic

Level of experience Intermediate

Sizes Small (medium, large)
Instructions are for size small. Changes for sizes medium and large are in parentheses.

Finished measurements
Bust at underarm 36 (39, 42)"
Length 22½ (23½, 24½)"

Gauge In pat st, 14 sts and 22 rows = 4" using larger needles.

PAT ST (multiple of 6 sts plus 3)

Rows 1 and 3 (RS) K.
Rows 2 and 4 P.
Row 5 P4, *yo, k1, yo, p5; rep from *, ending p4 instead of p5.
Row 6 K4, *p3, k5; rep from *, ending k4, instead of k5.
Row 7 P4, *k3, p5; rep from *, ending p4, instead of p5.
Row 8 K4, *p3 tog; k5, rep from *, ending k4 instead of k5.
Repeat rows 1 to 8 for pat st.

BACK

With larger needles, cast on 63 (69, 75) sts loosely. Work in garter st (k every row) for 3 rows. Work in pat st until piece measures 14½ (15, 15½)" from beg.

MATERIALS

- Judi & Co's ¼" ribbon (100% rayon, 100 yds each), 6 (7, 8) spools red
- Straight knitting needles sizes 9 and 10, or sizes to obtain gauge

SHAPE ARMHOLE AND NECK

Bind off 4 sts beg next 2 rows. Dec 1 st each end every other row 4 times—47 (53, 59) sts. Cont in pat st until armhole measures 8 (8½, 9)". Work across 12 (14, 16) sts, join a second spool of ribbon, work center 23 (25, 27) sts, and put on a holder, work across 12 (14, 16) sts. Put rem shoulder sts each side on stitch holder for three-needle bind-off or bind off these sts.

FRONT

Work same as back until armhole measures 5 (5¼, 5½)".

SHAPE NECK

Work across 15 (17, 19) sts, join a second spool of ribbon, work across center 17 (19, 21) sts and put on stitch holder, work rem 15 (17, 19) sts. Working both sides at once, dec 1 st at each neck edge every other row 3 times. When piece measures same as back, put 12 (14, 16) sts each side on stitch holder or bind off.

FINISHING

Block pieces to measurements, trying not to flatten out the "bubbles" in the pat st. Sew or k one shoulder tog.

NECKBAND

With RS facing and smaller needles, pick up 68 (72, 76) sts around neck edge, including sts on front and back holders. Work in garter st for 4 rows. Bind off loosely. Sew or k other shoulder and neckband tog.

ARMHOLE BANDS

With RS facing and larger needles, pick up 52 (56, 60) sts evenly around each armhole edge. Work in garter st for 4 rows. Bind off loosely.
Sew side seams, leaving 4" open at the bottom of sweater for slits.

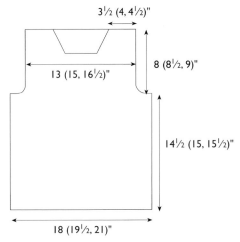

3½ (4, 4½)"

8 (8½, 9)"

13 (15, 16½)"

14½ (15, 15½)"

18 (19½, 21)"

White-on-White Striped Sweater

Level of experience Beginner

Sizes Petite (small, medium, large) Instructions are for size petite. Changes for sizes small, medium, and large are in parentheses.

Finished measurements
Bust at underarm 38 (41, 43, 46)"
Length 18 (19½, 21, 22½)"

Gauge In pat st, 10 sts and 16 rows = 4" using size 15 needles.

PAT ST

Rows 1 and 2 With CC, k.
Rows 3 and 5 (RS) With MC, k.
Rows 4 and 6 With MC, p.
Rep rows 1 to 6 for pat st.

BACK

With CC, cast on 48 (51, 54, 57) sts. Work in pat st for 8 (9, 10, 11)".

MATERIALS

- Judi & Co's ½" Rayon Ribbon (100% rayon, 100 yds each), 3 (4, 5, 5) spools (MC)
- Judi & Co's Rococo (144 yds each), 1 spool (CC) or ½" Rayon Ribbon, 1 (1, 1, 2) spools (CC)
- Straight knitting needles size 15, or size to obtain gauge
- Crochet hook size H

SHAPE SLEEVES

Inc 1 st each side every row 3 times—54 (57, 60, 63) sts. Work even until piece measures 14 (15, 16, 17)" from beg.

SHAPE NECK

Work 19 (20, 21, 22) sts, join second spool of ribbon and bind off center 16 (17, 18, 19) sts, work rem 19 (20, 21, 22) sts. Cont working both sides at same time with separate spools of ribbon, until piece measures 18 (19½, 21, 22½)" from beg. Bind off sts both sides or place 19 (20, 21, 22) sts on holders for three-needle bind-off.

FRONT

Work same as back.

FINISHING

Block pieces to measurements. Weave in all ends. Sew side seams. With RS facing, crochet hook and MC, work 1 row sc around neck edge.

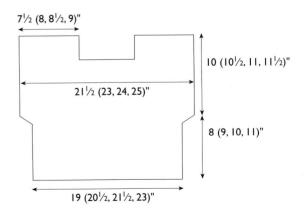

7½ (8, 8½, 9)"
10 (10½, 11, 11½)"
21½ (23, 24, 25)"
8 (9, 10, 11)"
19 (20½, 21½, 23)"

Bow Sweater

Level of experience Beginner

Sizes Small (medium, large, extra-large)
Instructions are for size small. Changes for
sizes medium, large, and extra-large are in
parentheses.

Finished measurements
Bust at underarm 38 (42, 45, 48)"
Length 18 (19, 19¾, 20¾)"

Gauge In St st, 10 sts and 14 rows = 4" using
size 15 needles.

Notes If using Fur, use a strand of Fur along
with ribbon every fourth row. (This will not
change the gauge.) Carry the Fur loosely up
the side. Do not cut at the end of each row.

BACK

Cast on 48 (52, 56, 60) sts with ribbon and Fur (if
desired). P1 row on WS. Work in St st until piece
measures 15½ (16½, 17¼, 18¼)" from beg.

MATERIALS

- Judi & Co.'s ½" Rayon Knitting Ribbon
  (100% rayon, 100 yds each), 3 (4, 5, 6)
  spools "Spring" Multicolor
- Straight knitting needles size 15, or size
  to obtain gauge
- Crochet hook size H
- Baruffa Fur 1 (2, 2, 2) balls White
  (optional)

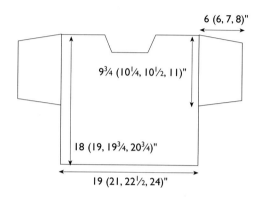

6 (6, 7, 8)"

9¾ (10¼, 10½, 11)"

18 (19, 19¾, 20¾)"

19 (21, 22½, 24)"

SHAPE NECK

Work 16 (18, 19, 21) sts, join a new strand of ribbon and bind off center 16 (16, 18, 18) sts, work
to end. Working both sides at the same time and
with separate ribbons, dec 1 st at each neck edge
on next row. Work even on rem 15 (17, 18, 20) sts
each side until piece measures 18 (19, 19¾, 20¾)",
or length desired. Bind off all sts, or put on stitch
holders for three-needle bind-off.

FRONT

Work same as back.

SLEEVES

Before working sleeves, sew or k tog shoulder
seams firmly to prevent stretching. Measure 9¾
(10¼, 10½, 11)" down from each side of shoulder
seam and place markers on sweater body. With
the RS facing, pick up and k48 (52, 54, 56) sts
evenly spaced between markers. Work in St st, dec
1 st each side every fourth row 4 (5, 6, 6) times.
Work even until sleeve measures 6 (6, 7, 8)" from
beg. Bind off rem 40 (42, 42, 44) sts knitwise.

FINISHING

Block pieces to measurements. Sew side and sleeve seams. Cut 26 pieces of ribbon approx 5" long. Tie these at random on front and back, and on the sleeves of the sweater. (Cut on the diagonal to prevent raveling.)

With the RS facing using crochet hook, work 1 row of sc around neck edge. Weave in loose ends.

SUGGESTION

This style sweater can be worked in a solid color or in a stripe of several colors.

A Bit o' Lace

Level of experience Intermediate

Sizes Small (medium, large)
Instructions are for size small. Changes for sizes medium and large are in parentheses.

Finished measurements
Bust at underarm 36 (39, 42)"
Length 18 (19, 20)"

Gauge In St st, 11 sts and 14 rows = 4" using larger needles.

Note This sweater has a lot of "give."

WAVE ST (multiple of 12 sts plus 1)
Rows 1 to 4 K.
Rows 5, 7, 9, 11 (RS) K1, *[k2 tog] twice, [yo, k1] 3 times, yo, [SSK] twice, k1*; rep from * to end.
Rows 6, 8, 10, 12 P.

BACK

With smaller needles, cast on 73 sts for all sizes. Work 12 rows wave st.
Row 13 Dec 23 (19, 15) sts evenly across—50 (54, 58) sts. Change to larger needles and work in St st (k on RS, p on WS) until piece measures 18 (19, 20)" from beg. (Measure to bottom of scallop.) Bind off loosely.

RIGHT FRONT

With smaller needles, cast on 37 sts for all sizes. Work same as back, dec 12 (10, 8) sts evenly across row 13—25 (27, 29) sts. Work even until piece measures 8½ (9, 9½)" from beg.

MATERIALS
- Judi & Co's Rayon Luminesse Ribbon (100 yds each), 5 (5, 6) skeins
- Straight knitting needles sizes 11 and 13, or sizes to obtain gauge
- One ¾" diameter button

SHAPE V-NECK

Dec 1 st at neck edge on next row, then every fourth row 7 (7, 8) times more—17 (19, 20) sts. Work even until piece measures 18 (19, 20)" from beg. Bind off all sts.

LEFT FRONT

Work to correspond to right front, reversing all shaping.

SLEEVES

With smaller needles, cast on 49 sts for all sizes. Work 12 rows wave st.
Row 13 Dec 8 (8, 4) sts evenly across row—41 (41, 45) sts. Work in St st for 2 rows and bind off loosely.

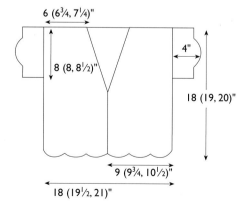

FRONT BORDER

With RS facing and smaller needles, pick up and
k40 (42, 45) sts along right front edge, 16 (16, 18)
sts along back neck, and 40 (42, 45) sts along left
front edge—96 (100, 108) sts.

Next row (WS) K to last 20 (21, 22) sts, bind off
2 sts for buttonhole, k to end. K next row, casting
on 2 sts over bound-off sts. K1 row. Bind off all sts
loosely.

FINISHING

Block pieces to measurements. Sew shoulder
seams. Place markers 8 (8, 8½)" down from shoulders on front and back for armholes. Sew bound-
off edge of sleeve between markers. Sew side and
sleeve seams. Sew on button to correspond with
buttonhole.

Cropped Tank Top

Level of experience Beginner

Sizes Petite (small, medium, large)
Instructions are for size petite. Changes
for sizes small, medium, and large are in
parentheses.

Finished measurements
Bust at underarm 36 (39, 41, 44)"
Length 16½ (17½, 19, 20½)"

Gauge In St st, 10 sts and 16 rows = 4" using
size 15 needles.

BACK

With size 15 needles, cast on 46 (49, 52, 55) sts.
P1 row on WS. Work in rev St st (p on RS, k on
WS) until piece measures 8 (9, 10, 11)" from beg.

SHAPE ARMHOLE

Bind off 3 sts at beg of next 2 rows. Dec 1 st each
end every other row 4 times—32 (35, 38, 41) sts.
Work even until armhole measures 4 (4, 4½, 4½)",
end with a WS row.

MATERIALS

- Judi & Co's ½" Rayon Knitting Ribbon
  (100% rayon, 100 yds each), 3 (4, 4, 5)
  spools
- Straight knitting needles size 15, or size
  to obtain gauge

SHAPE NECK

Next row (RS) K10 (11, 12, 13), join a second
spool of ribbon and bind off center 12 (13, 14, 15)
sts, k to end. Working both sides at the same time,
dec 1 st at each neck edge every other row
3 (4, 4, 5) times—7 (7, 8, 8) sts each side. Work
even until armhole measures 8½ (8½, 9, 9½)".
Bind off sts or put sts on stitch holders for
three-needle bind-off.

FRONT

Work same as back.

FINISHING

Block pieces to measurements. Sew shoulder and
side seams.

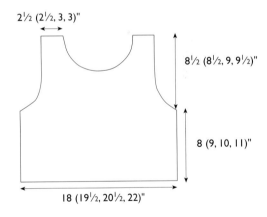

2½ (2½, 3, 3)"

8½ (8½, 9, 9½)"

8 (9, 10, 11)"

18 (19½, 20½, 22)"

Sleeveless Jacket

Level of experience Beginner

Sizes Petite (small, medium, large)
Instructions are for size petite. Changes for sizes small, medium, and large are in parentheses.

Finished measurements
Bust at underarm 39 (41½, 43½, 45½)"
Length 24 (25, 26, 27)"

Gauge In St st, 10 sts and 16 rows = 4" using larger needles.

BACK

With larger needles and MC, cast on 48 (51, 54, 57) sts. Work in St st (k on RS, p on WS) for 14 (15, 16, 16)", end with a WS row.

SHAPE ARMHOLE

Bind off 3 sts at beg of next 2 rows. Dec 1 st each end every other row 3 times—36 (39, 42, 45) sts. Work even until armhole measures 10 (10, 11, 11)". Bind off or put sts on stitch holders for three-needle bind-off.

MATERIALS

- Judi & Co's ½" Rayon Knitting Ribbon (100% rayon, 100 yds each), 4 (5, 5, 6) spools Ecru (MC); 1 spool each Turquoise (A), Winter Plum (B), and Coral (C)
- Straight knitting needles sizes 10½ and 15, or sizes to obtain gauge
- Crochet hook size F
- Six 1" diameter buttons

RIGHT FRONT

With larger needles and MC, cast on 26 (27, 28, 29) sts. Work same as back until piece measures 14 (15, 16, 16)" from beg, end with a RS row.

SHAPE ARMHOLE

Next row (WS) Bind off 3 sts at beg of next row (armhole edge) and cont to dec 1 st at armhole edge every other row 3 times—20 (21, 22, 23) sts. Work even until armhole measures 6", end with a WS row.

SHAPE NECK

Next row (RS) Bind off 4 sts (neck edge), work to end. Cont to dec 1 st at neck edge every other row 3 times—13 (14, 15, 16) sts. Work even until piece measures same length as back. Bind off or put sts on a stitch holder.

LEFT FRONT

Work to correspond to right front, reversing all shaping. Sew shoulder seams.

COLLAR

With smaller needles and B, pick up and k42 (46, 50, 54) sts around neck edge. Work in St st for 1". Change to larger needles and cont in St st for 1", and then bind off. This will roll back, and p side will show.

ARMHOLE BANDS

With RS facing, smaller needles, and A for one armhole, C for second armhole, pick up and k58 (58, 64, 64) sts around each armhole edge and work in St st for 1½". Bind off loosely.

POCKETS

LOWER RIGHT

With A and larger needles, cast on 15 sts and work in rev St st (p on RS, k on WS) for 5". Join C and work in St st for 3 rows. Bind off loosely.

LOWER LEFT

Follow directions for previous pocket, using B for pocket and A for top trim.

UPPER LEFT

With larger needles and C, cast on 10 sts. Work in rev St st for 5". Bind off loosely.

FINISHING

Block pieces to measurements. Sew side seams, leaving 5" opening at lower edge for slits. Sew shoulder seams or k tog.
Refer to drawing for pocket placement. Top of top left pocket is on same level as armhole bind-off. Whipstitch pockets on sweater with matching ribbon. With crochet hook and MC, work 2 rows of sc down front of sweater. Work 1 row sc around slits on sides.

OPTIONAL

Work six buttonholes in last row of sc on right front, spacing them evenly apart. Sew on buttons.

Sleeveless Jacket

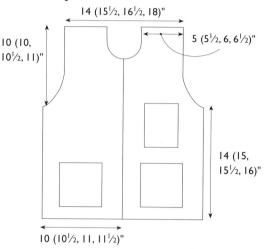

14 (15½, 16½, 18)"

10 (10, 10½, 11)"

5 (5½, 6, 6½)"

14 (15, 15½, 16)"

10 (10½, 11, 11½)"

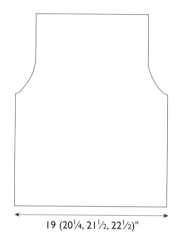

19 (20¼, 21½, 22½)"

Cabled Twinset

Level of experience Intermediate

Sizes Petite (small, medium, large)
Instructions are for size petite. Changes
for sizes small, medium, and large are in
parentheses.

Finished measurements
Bust at underarm (cardigan and sleeveless
shell) 35½ (37½, 39½, 41½)" (This is a
close-fitting sweater.)
Length (cardigan) 19 (20, 21, 22)"
(sleeveless shell) 18 (19, 20, 21)"

Gauge In St st, 16 sts and 20 rows = 4" using
larger needles.

8-ST CABLE

Rows 1 and 5 (RS) K.
Row 2 and all WS rows P.

MATERIALS

- **Cardigan:** Judi & Co.'s ¼" Rayon Ribbon
  (100% rayon, 100 yds each), 9 (10, 10,
  11) spools
- Six "mother-of-pearl" or decorative but-
  tons ⅝" diameter
- **Sleeveless shell:** Judi & Co.'s ¼" Rayon
  Ribbon (100% rayon, 100 yds each), 4
  (4, 5, 5) spools
- Straight knitting needles sizes 8 and 10½,
  or sizes to obtain gauge
- Circular needle size 8
- Cable needle

Rows 3 and 7 Sl 4 sts to cn and hold to back of
work, k4, k4 from cn.

6-ST CABLE

Rows 1 and 5 (RS) K.
Row 2 and all WS rows P.
Rows 3 and 7 Sl 3 sts to cn and hold to back of
work, k3, k3 from cn.

4-ST CABLE

Rows 1 and 5 (RS) K.
Row 2 and all WS rows P.
Rows 3 and 7 Sl 2 sts to cn and hold to back of
work, k2, k2 from cn.

BACK (cardigan)

With smaller needles, cast on 64 (68, 72, 76) sts.
Work in k1, p1 rib for 2½", inc 6 sts evenly across
last row—70 (74, 78, 82) sts. Change to larger
needles and work as follows:
Row 1 (RS) P15 (16, 17, 18), work 8-st cable, p24
(26, 28, 30), work 8-st cable, p15 (16, 17, 18). Cont
as established, working sts outside of cables in rev
St st (p on RS, k on WS) for 7 rows more.
Row 9 (RS) P16 (17, 18, 19), work 6-st cable, p26
(28, 30, 32), work 6-st cable, p16 (17, 18, 19). Cont
as established for 7 rows more.
Row 17 P17 (18, 19, 20), work 4-st cable, p28 (30,
32, 34), work 4-st cable, p17 (18, 19, 20). Cont as
established for 7 rows more.
Row 25 P.
Cont in rev St st on all sts until piece measures 11
(11½, 12, 12½)" from beg.

SHAPE ARMHOLE

Bind off 4 sts beg of next 2 rows. Dec 1 st each
end every other row 2 (3, 4, 5) times—58 (60, 62,
64) sts. Work even until armhole measures

8 (8½, 9, 9½)". Bind off 14 (15, 15, 16) sts at beg of next 2 rows. Place rem 30 (30, 32, 32) sts on a holder for back neck.

LEFT FRONT (cardigan)

With smaller needles, cast on 36 (38, 40, 42) sts. Work in k1, p1 rib for 2½", inc 2 sts on last row—38 (40, 42, 44) sts. Change to larger needles and work as follows:

Row 1 (RS) P15, (16, 17, 18), work 8-st cable, p9 (10, 11, 12), cont rib over last 6 sts for front border.

Work cables same as back, then cont in rev St st on all sts until same length as back to armhole. Shape armhole same as back. Work even until armhole measures 5 (5½, 6, 6½)", end with a RS row.

SHAPE NECK

Next row (WS) Bind off 6 sts of border plus 7 (7, 8, 8) sts (neck edge), work to end. Dec 1 st at neck edge every other row 5 times. When same length as back, bind off rem 14 (15, 15, 16) sts for shoulder.

Place markers on front band for 5 buttons, the first one ½" from lower edge, the last one 2½" from top edge, and 3 others spaced evenly between.

RIGHT FRONT (cardigan)

Work same as left front, reversing shaping and working buttonholes opposite markers as follows: At beg of a RS row, rib 3, yo, k2 tog, work to end.

SLEEVES (cardigan)

With smaller needles, cast on 32 (34, 36, 38) sts. Work in k1, p1 rib for 2½", inc 8 sts evenly spaced across last row—40 (42, 44, 46) sts. Change to larger needles and work in rev St st, inc 1 st each end every 1½" 8 times—56 (58, 60, 62) sts. Work even until piece measures 15½ (16, 16½, 17)" from beg.

SHAPE CAP

Bind off 4 sts at beg of next 2 rows. Dec 1 st each end every other row 9 (10, 11, 12) times. Bind off 2 sts at beg of next 12 rows. Bind off rem 6 sts.

FINISHING (cardigan)

Block pieces to measurement. Sew shoulder and side seams. Set in sleeves.

NECKBAND

With RS facing and smaller needles, pick up 6 sts of rib from right front, 14 (14, 15, 15) sts along right front neck, 30 (30, 32, 32) sts along back neck, 14 (14, 15, 15) sts along left from neck, and 6 rib sts from left front—70 (70, 74, 74) sts. Work in k1, p1 rib for ½". Make another buttonhole as before. Rib until band measures 1¼". Bind off loosely. Sew on buttons.

BACK (sleeveless shell)

With smaller needles, cast on 64 (68, 72, 76) sts. Work in k1, p1 rib for 2½", inc 6 sts evenly across last row—70 (74, 78, 82) sts. Change to larger needles and work in rev St st until piece measures 10 (10½, 11, 11½)" from beg.

SHAPE ARMHOLE

Bind off 4 sts at beg of next 2 rows. Dec 1 st each end every other row 3 (4, 5, 6) times—56 (58, 60, 62) sts. Work even until armhole measures 7½ (8, 8½, 9)".

SHAPE NECK

Work 13 (14, 14, 15) sts, join second length of ribbon, work center 30 (30, 32, 32) sts and slip onto a stitch holder for neck, work rem 13 (14, 14, 15) sts. Working both sides at once, work even until armhole measures 8 (8½, 9, 9½)". Bind off rem sts each side for shoulders.

FRONT (sleeveless shell)

Cast on and work rib and inc row same as back— 70 (74, 78, 82) sts. Change to larger needles and work cables same as cardigan back, then cont in rev St st on all sts until piece measures 10 (10½, 11, 11½)" from beg. Shape armhole same as back—56 (58, 60, 63) sts. Work even until armhole measures 5 (5½, 6, 6½)".

SHAPE NECK

Work 19 (20, 20, 21) sts, join second length of ribbon, slip center 18 (18, 20, 20) sts to a holder; work rem 19 (20, 20, 21) sts. Working both sides at once, bind off from each neck edge 3 sts once, 2 sts once, 1 st once. When same length as back, bind off rem 13 (14, 14, 15) sts each side for shoulders.

FINISHING (sleeveless shell)

Block pieces to measurements. Sew shoulder and side seams.

ARMHOLE BANDS

With RS facing and circular needle, pick up 68 (72, 76, 80) sts evenly around each armhole. Join and work in k1, p1 rib for 1". Bind off loosely.

NECKBAND

With RS facing and circular needle, pick up 68 (68, 72, 72) sts around neck edge. Join and work in k1, p1 rib for 1". Bind off loosely.

Cabled Twinset
Cardigan

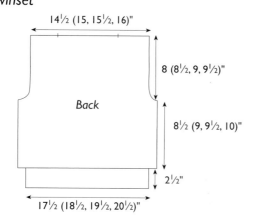

14½ (15, 15½, 16)"

8 (8½, 9, 9½)"

Back

8½ (9, 9½, 10)"

2½"

17½ (18½, 19½, 20½)"

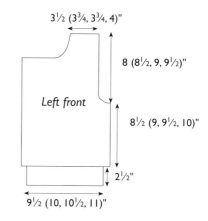

3½ (3¾, 3¾, 4)"

8 (8½, 9, 9½)"

Left front

8½ (9, 9½, 10)"

2½"

9½ (10, 10½, 11)"

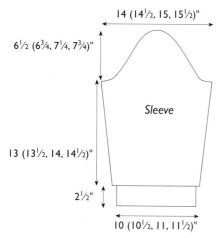

14 (14½, 15, 15½)"

6½ (6¾, 7¼, 7¾)"

Sleeve

13 (13½, 14, 14½)"

2½"

10 (10½, 11, 11½)"

Sleeveless shell

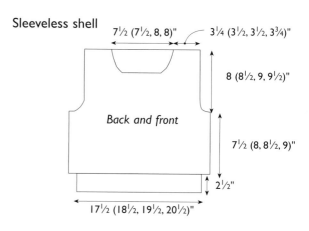

7½ (7½, 8, 8)"   3¼ (3½, 3½, 3¾)"

8 (8½, 9, 9½)"

Back and front

7½ (8, 8½, 9)"

2½"

17½ (18½, 19½, 20½)"

White-on-White V-Neck Sweater

Level of experience Intermediate

Sizes Small (medium, large)
Instructions are for size small. Changes for sizes medium and large are in parentheses.

Finished measurements
Bust at underarm 41 (44, 47)"
Length 23 (23½, 24)"

Gauge In pat I, 14 sts and 19 rows = 4" using size 10½ circular needle.

Note This sweater is worked back and forth on a circular needle.

PAT I

Row 1 (RS) With A, k. Push sts back to beg of needle.
Row 2 (RS) With B, k and turn work.
Row 3 (WS) With A, p. Push sts back to beg of needle.

MATERIALS

- Judi & Co.'s ½" Rayon Ribbon
  (100% rayon, 100 yds each),
  4 (4, 5) spools White (A)
- Judi & Co.'s Petite Satin Cord
  (70 yds each), 5 (5, 6) spools White (B)
- Judi & Co.'s ¼" Acetate Satin Ribbon
  (100 yds each, double-faced),
  approx 25 yds White (C)
- Straight knitting needles size 8
- Circular knitting needles sizes 8 and 10½
- Stitch marker

Row 4 (WS) With B, p and turn work.
Rep rows 1 to 4 for pat I.

PAT II

Row 1 (RS) With C, *k1, yo; rep from * to end.
Row 2 With C, p, dropping each yo.

BACK

With straight needles and B, cast on 64 (70, 74) sts. Work in k1, p1 rib for 4 rows. Change to larger circular needle and inc 8 sts evenly across next row and working pat I for 2 rows—72 (78, 82) sts. Work pat II for 2 rows. Work pat I for 4 rows. Work pat II for 2 rows. Cont pat I until piece measures 23 (23½, 24)" from beg, or length desired. Bind off all sts loosely.

FRONT

Work same as back until piece measures 14 (14½, 14½)" from beg.

SHAPE NECK

Work 36 (39, 41) sts, join second spool of ribbon, work to end. Working both sides at same time with separate spools, dec 1 st at each neck edge every other row 7 (9, 8) times, every fourth row 6 (5, 6) times. Work even until piece measures same length as back. Bind off rem 23 (25 27) sts loosely each side for shoulders.

SLEEVES

With straight needles and B, cast on 26 sts. Work in k1, p1 rib for 4 rows.
Change to larger circular needle and work pat I for 2 rows. Work pat II for 2 rows. Work pat I for 4 rows. Work pat II for 2 rows. Cont with pat I, *at the same time*, inc 1 st each side every other row 10 (11, 15) times, every fourth row 10 (10, 8)

times—66 (70, 74) sts. Work even until piece measures 16½ (17, 17)" from beg, or length desired. Bind off all sts loosely.

FINISHING

Sew shoulder seams. Place markers 9½ (10, 10½)" down from shoulder seams on front and back for armholes. Sew top of sleeves between markers. Sew side and sleeve seams.

NECKBAND

With RS facing, smaller circular needle, and B, pick up and k26 (28, 28) sts along back neck, 36 (36, 38) sts along left front neck, 1 st at center front, and mark this st, pick up 36 (36, 38) sts along right front neck—99 (101, 105) sts. Join and work in k1, p1 rib, keeping center st as a k st, and dec 1 st each side of center st every row for 4 rows. Bind off in rib.

White-on-White V-Neck Sweater

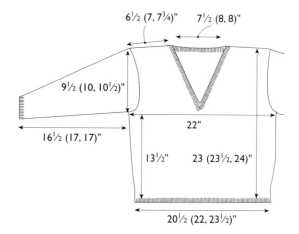

6½ (7, 7¾)"   7½ (8, 8)"

9½ (10, 10½)"

16½ (17, 17)"

22"

13½"   23 (23½, 24)"

20½ (22, 23½)"

Lace Chevron Cardigan

Level of experience Intermediate

Sizes Small (medium, large)
Instructions are for size small. Changes for
sizes medium and large are in parentheses.

Finished measurements
Bust at underarm 36½ (40½, 44½)"
Length 17½ (18, 19½)"

Gauge In lace pat, 10 sts = 4" and 10 rows =
3" using size 15 needles.

Note Sweater is worked in one piece until
armhole (see the photo on p. 52).

LACE PAT (multiple of 10 sts plus I)
Row 1 and every WS row P.
Row 2 *K5, yo, SSK, k3; rep from *, end k1.
Row 4 *K3, k2 tog, yo, k1, yo, SSK, k2; rep from *,
end k1.
Row 6 *K2, k2 tog, yo, k3, yo, SSK, k1; rep from *,
end k1.
Row 8 *K1, k2 tog, yo k5, yo, SSK; rep from *,
end k1.
Row 10 K2 tog, yo, k7, * yo, sl 1—k2 tog—psso,
yo, k7; rep from *, end yo, SSK.
Rep rows 1 to 10 for lace pat.

MATERIALS
- Judi & Co's Rayon Luminesse (100 yds
  each), 5 (6, 7) skeins Brown Iris
- Straight knitting needles sizes 11, 13, 15,
  or sizes to obtain gauge
- Three 1" diameter buttons

BODY
With size 13 needles, cast on 88 (96, 104) sts.
Work in garter st (k every row) for 4 rows. P1
row, inc 3 (5, 7) sts evenly across—91 (101, 111)
sts. Change to size 15 needles and work in lace
pat until piece measures 9 (9, 10)" from beg, end
with a RS row.

DIVIDE FOR FRONTS AND BACK
Next row (WS) P22 (25, 27) for left front and
place on a stitch holder, p47 (51, 57) for back,
place rem 22 (25, 27) sts on a second holder for
right front. Work on back sts only until 30 rows of
lace pat have been worked, then cont in St st (k
on RS, p on WS) on all sts until piece measures
17½ (18, 19½)" from beg. Bind off 15 (17, 19) sts
at beg of next 2 rows, or place on stitch holder
for three-needle bind-off. Bind off rem 17 (17, 19)
sts for back neck.
Sl 22 (25, 27) sts from left front holder to needle
to work next row from RS.

SHAPE V-NECK

Next row (RS) Work to last 2 sts, dec 1 st (neck edge). Cont to dec 1 st at neck edge every third row 6 (7, 7) times, *at the same time*, when 30 rows of lace pat have been worked, cont in St st on all sts. Work even until same length as back. Bind off rem 15 (17, 19) sts or place on stitch holder for three-needle bind-off. Work right front to correspond to left front, reversing shaping.

SLEEVES

With size 13 needles, cast on 20 (22, 24) sts. Work in garter st for 4 rows, inc 11 (9, 7) sts evenly across last row—31 sts. Change to size 15 needles and work in lace pat, inc 1 st each end (working inc sts into St st) every sixth row 6 (7, 8) times—43 (45, 47) sts. Work even until piece measures 17 (17½, 18)" from beg. Bind off loosely.

FINISHING

Block pieces to measurements. Sew shoulder seams or k tog. Set in sleeves.

OUTSIDE EDGING

With RS facing and size 11 needles, pick up 24 (24, 28) sts along right front to first neck dec, 24 (26, 28) sts to shoulder, 17 (17, 19) sts along back of neck, 24 (26, 28) sts to first dec on left front, 24 (24, 28) sts down left front. K1 row and bind off. Sew buttons evenly along left front between lower edge and beg of V-neck. Eyelets in lace pat serve as buttonholes.

Lace Chevron Cardigan

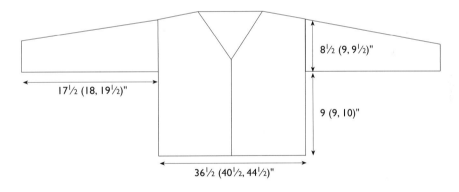

Wide-Ribbed Turtleneck

Level of experience Intermediate

Sizes Petite (small, medium, large)
Instructions are for size petite. Changes
for sizes small, medium, and large are in
parentheses.

Finished measurements
Bust at underarm 34 (36½, 38½, 41½)"
Length 17 (17½, 18½, 19)"

Gauge In k2, p3 rib (slightly stretched), 16 sts
and 18 rows = 4" using larger needles.

K2, P3 RIB

Row 1 (RS) *K2, p3; rep from * to end.
Row 2 K the knit sts and p the purl sts.
Rep row 2 for k2, p3 rib.

BACK

With smaller needles, cast on 68 (73, 77, 83) sts.

MATERIALS

- Judi & Co.'s Winter Plum (70 yds each), 8
  (9, 10, 11) spools
- Straight knitting needles sizes 8 and 10,
  or sizes to obtain gauge
- Circular needles sizes 8 to 16

BEG K2, P3 RIB

Row 1 (RS) P3 (3, 0, 3), *k2, p3; rep from *, end
k0 (0, 2, 0). Cont in rib as established for 1".
Change to larger needles and cont rib until piece
measures 8 (8½, 9, 9½)" from beg.

SHAPE ARMHOLES

When shaping, be sure to maintain rib pat. Bind off
4 (4, 4, 5) sts at beg of next 2 rows. Dec 1 st each
end every other row 3 (4, 5, 6) times—54 (57, 59,
61) sts. Work even until piece measures 16½ (17,
18, 18½)" from beg.

SHAPE NECK

Work 15 (16, 17, 17) sts, sl next 24 (25, 25, 27) sts
to a stitch holder, join second ball, work rem 15
(16, 17, 17) sts. On next row, dec 1 st at each
neck edge—14 (15, 16, 16) sts rem on each side.
When piece measures 17 (17½, 18½, 19)" from
beg, bind off or place on holder for three-needle
bind-off.

FRONT

Work same as back until piece measures 15 (15½,
16½, 17)" from beg.

SHAPE NECK

Work 17 (18, 19, 19) sts, sl next 20 (21, 21, 23)
sts to a stitch holder, join second ball, work rem

Wide-Ribbed Turtleneck

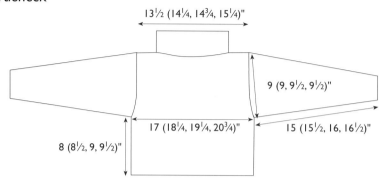

13½ (14¼, 14¾, 15¼)"

9 (9, 9½, 9½)"

17 (18¼, 19¼, 20¾)"

15 (15½, 16, 16½)"

8 (8½, 9, 9½)"

17 (18, 19, 19) sts. Working both sides at the same time, dec 1 st at each neck edge every other row 3 times—14 (15, 16, 16) sts each side. Work even until piece measures 17 (17½, 18½, 19)" from beg. Bind off or place on holder for three-needle bind-off.

SLEEVES

With larger needles, cast on 28 (28, 32, 32) sts. **Beg k2, p3 rib—Row 1 (RS)** P3 (3, 0, 0), *k2, p3; rep from *, end k0 (0, 2, 2). Cont in rib as established, inc 1 st each end (working inc sts into rib) every sixth row 10 (11, 11, 12) times—48 (50, 54, 56) sts. Work even until piece measures 15 (15½, 16, 16½)" from beg.

SHAPE CAP

Bind off 3 (3, 4, 4) sts at beg of next 2 rows. Dec 1 st each end every other row until cap measures 5¾ (6¼, 6¾, 7¼)". Bind off rem sts.

FINISHING

Block pieces to measurements. Sew or k shoulders tog. Set in sleeves. Sew side and sleeve seams.

COLLAR

With RS facing and circular needle, beg at shoulder seam, pick up 60 (65, 65, 70) sts around neck edge, including sts on holders. Work in k2, p3 rib, making sure that ribs from holders cont straight up from body into collar, for 5". Bind off *loosely* in rib.

Granny Square Vest

Level of experience Intermediate

Sizes Small (medium, large)
Instructions are for size small. Changes for sizes medium and large are in parentheses.

Finished measurements
Bust at underarm (closed) 34¼ (37¾, 41¼)"
Length 18½ (20, 21½)"

Gauge I granny square = 4½"

Note Vest can also be worked in only three colors, like the Patchwork Drawstring Bag on page 94. If worked with three colors, you will need 3 (3, 4) spools MC, 2 spools A, and I spool B.

BASIC GRANNY SQUARE

Foundation ch rnd Ch 6, join with a sl st to form a ring.
Rnd I Ch 3 (counts as I dc), in ring work: 2 dc, ch 3, [3 dc, ch 3] 3 times, join with a sl st.
Rnd 2 Sl st to first sp (ch 3, 2 dc, ch 3, 3 dc) into first ch-3 sp (ch I, 3 dc, ch 3, 3 dc) into each corner; rep from *, ending ch I, join with a sl st.
Rnd 3 Sl st to first sp (ch 2, 2 dc, ch 3, 3 dc) into first ch-3 sp, *ch I, 3 dc into ch-1 sp (ch I, 3 dc, ch 3, 3 dc) into next corner; rep from *, end ch I, join with a sl st. Fasten off.
Rnd 4 Rep rnd 3, adding an extra 3 dc on each side. join with a sl st and fasten off.

BODY

Make 14 squares as follows: Work ch ring and first 3 rnds using colors indicated on placement diagram. Work the fourth rnd of every square with MC. With MC, work 0 (1, 2) rnds sc around

each square. Sl st squares tog following placement diagram on p. 59.

STRAPS

Make 5 (6, 6) squares for each strap as follows: Work ch ring and first rnd using color indicated on placement diagram and work the second rnd of every square with MC. Join squares same as body. On the last square, work rows of dc with MC until strap measures 18 (19, 20)" from beg. Fasten off.

FINISHING

With RS facing and MC, work I rnd sc around entire outside edge of body. Sew straps to body (see diagram below for placement: 2¼" sections represent placement of straps).

NOTE

Sew dc edge of straps to back.

TIES (MAKE 6)

With MC, ch 24 and sl st in second ch from hook and in each ch to end. Fasten off. Attach ties to fronts.

MATERIALS

- Judi & Co's Satin Cord (144 yds each), 3 (3, 4) spools Black (MC); I spool each Brown (A), Olive (B), Orange (C), Pink (D), Blue (E), Red (F), Purple (G), and Gold (H)
- Crochet hook size G, or size to obtain gauge

Placement Diagrams

Right strap

B
D
F
E
H
C

Left strap

G
F
D
B
F
E

For sizes M and L only

Body

E,C,B	G,D,E	D,A,F	F,G,H	G,F,B	H,G,F	A,D,E
F,B,E	C,B,H	F,H,G	H,G,F	F,G,A	B,D,E	C,B,A

3 (3½, 4)"   6 (7, 7¾)"

2¼"

Left front	Back	Right front

9½ (10½, 11½)"

8¼ (9¼, 10)"   16½ (18½, 20¼)"

Chapter 2

BAGS

I loved designing the bags in this chapter. They work up quickly (most can be finished in a weekend) and are fun to embellish. From small evening bags to casual back-packs, there is something to entice the beginner to experienced knitter or crocheter.

Ribbon and Satin Cord Sling

Finished measurements
Approx 6½" wide by 7½" tall, with drawstring pulled taut
Bottom of bag 5" diameter

BAG

With Satin Cord, ch 6. Join with a sl st to form ring.

BOTTOM

Rnd 1 Work 12 sc in ring.
Rnd 2 Inc 1 st in every sc—24 sc.
Rnd 3 Inc 1 st in every third sc.
Rnd 4 Inc 1 st in every fourth sc.
Rnd 5 Inc 1 st in every fifth sc.
Rnd 6 Inc 1 st in every sixth sc.
Rnd 7 Inc 1 st in every seventh sc.
Rnd 8 Inc 1 st in every eighth sc.
Work even without inc until diameter of bottom of bag measures 5". (Make sure bottom remains flat as you are working.)

SIDES

Change to ½" ribbon. Work sc for 3 rnds.
*Change to Satin Cord. Work sc for 2 rnds.
Change to ½" ribbon. Work sc for 2 rnds*. Rep between *s (4 rnds), ending with ½" ribbon section, until bag measures approx 7" high. Work 1 rnd dc in Satin Cord for drawstring. Finish with 1 more rnd of sc or 1 rnd of crab st (backwards crochet, from left to right).

DRAWSTRING

Using Satin Cord, ch until piece measures 36". Sl st along ch, fasten off, and cut cord. Draw cord through dc rnd so back and front are flat and there is an inverted pleat on each side. Bring ends to front and tie.
If preferred, you can make a twisted cord: Cut a 4-yd piece of Satin Cord. Lp one end over a door knob or something stationary. Twist this single cord very tightly. It will double onto itself. Knot ends of cord together and draw through dc rnd as described for crocheted cord.

SLING

Using ½" ribbon, ch 116 or until 38" (or length desired). Sc along this ch. Attach to bottom back of bag where ribbon joins the Satin Cord bottom. Attach other end of strap to front of bag in top of ribbon section and directly under the Satin Cord drawstring. Place plastic canvas in bottom of bag.

MATERIALS

- Judi & Co.'s ½" Rayon Knitting Ribbon (100% Rayon, 100 yds each), 1 spool
- Judi & Co.'s Satin Cord (144 yds each), 1 spool
- Crochet hook size G
- 5" diameter plastic canvas (6" cut to size) or 4½" diameter

Flower Bag

Crocheted version

Finished measurements
10½" wide by 7" tall, from under handle

Gauge In sc, 14 sts = 4" using size F crochet hook.

BAG (make 2 pieces)
With MC, work approx 82 sc tightly around ring to cover (see page 5). Join with a sl st, ch 1, turn.
Rnd 1 Sc in each of next 30 sts, ch 1, turn. Cont to work sc in rows (ch 1, turn at end of every row), inc 1 st each end every row 3 times—36 sts. Work even in sc until piece measures 7". Fasten off.

FINISHING
Whipstitch sides and bottom tog starting with last inc row on side (leaving 1½" opening).

STEM
With CC, ch 11 and work sl st along ch.

FLOWER
Ch 6. Join with a sl st. Work 16 dc in center of ring. Join with a sl st.

Next rnd [Ch 3, sk 1 st, sc in next st] 8 times (8 lps).
Next rnd *Sc in lp, 3 dc in same lp, sc in same lp; rep from * and join to first lp.
Leaving approx ½ yd, break the raffia. Thread needle and go through the middle dc of each petal. Draw in and sew on bag. Make button center and sew on. Tack stem in same manner (see the drawing on page 66).

BUTTON
Ch 4. Join with a sl st to form ring.
Rnd 1 Work 8 sc in ring.
Rnd 2 Sc in each sc.
Rnd 3 Work 2 sc tog around—4 sc. Cut raffia about 8" long. Stuff button with raffia. Thread needle and draw tightly through this row.

BUTTON LP
Attach raffia with sl st to center bottom of ring. Ch17. Fold in half and attach with sl st to inside of bag. Weave in any loose ends. Sew on button.

STEAMING
Finished bag must be steamed lightly and pulled into shape. Lay flat to dry. Be sure to use pressing cloth over bag.

Knitted version

Finished measurements
8" wide by 7" tall, from under the handle

Gauge In garter st, 18 sts and 36 rows = 4" using size 7 needles.

MATERIALS (crocheted)
- Judi & Co.'s Rayon Raffia (72 yds each), 3 skeins MC, 1 skein CC
- Two 4" diameter metal rings
- Crochet hook size F
- Yarn needle

BAG (make 2 pieces)

With MC, work 82 sc tightly around ring to cover. Join with a sl st, ch 1, turn.

Rnd 1 Sc in each of next 28 sts.

With circular needle, pick up 28 sts along sc just worked. K1 row. Cont in garter st (k every row), inc 1 st each end every other row 5 times—38 sts. Work even until piece measures 7" from top. Bind off.

FINISHING

Sl st bottom and sides tog on WS up to last inc, leaving approx 1½" opening at the top on each side.

STEM AND FLOWER (1 cord)

With dp knitting needles, cast on 3 stitches. K3.

MATERIALS (knitted)

- Judi & Co.'s Rayon Raffia (72 yds each), 2 skeins MC
- Trim (optional): Judi & Co.'s Rayon Raffia, 1 skein CC; two dp knitting needles size 7
- Two 4" diameter metal rings
- Crochet hook size D
- Circular needle size 7, or size to obtain gauge
- Straight needles size 7, if desired
- Lining fabric (optional)
- One ¾" diameter button

*Do not turn. Slide the sts to right end of the needle and k3; rep from *. This will form a tube. (Yarn is pulled across the back of the row.) Cont until tube measures approx 30" in length. Do not bind off. Pin cord onto bag (starting with cast-on edge) as in the photo on page 64. Adjust length of cord and bind off when proper length. Tack down with same color raffia as cord.

BUTTON

Sew on button or make a crochet button as in the crochet version on page 65.

Crochet Flower Pattern

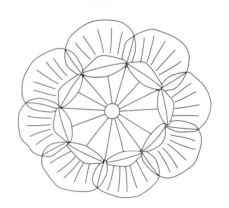

Drawstring Bags

Finished measurements
About 8" tall, 5" diameter

Gauge
Working rnds of sc, 3 sts and 4 rnds = 1" using size G crochet hook.

Note
Four different versions of this bag can be made:
• Basic Drawstring Bag without embellishments
• Drawstring Bag with Bobbles
• Drawstring Bag with Bobbles, Beads, and Fringe ("cement" version shown)
• "Wedding Cake" Drawstring Bag (with Dazzle ribbon)

BASIC DRAWSTRING BAG

Beg with the base of bag, ch 4. Join with a sl st to form ring.
Rnd 1 Ch 1, work 8 sc in ring.
Rnd 2 Work 2 sc in each sc—16 sc.
Rnd 3 *Sc in next sc, 2 sc in next sc; rep from * around—24 sc.

MATERIALS

• Judi & Co.'s ¼" Knitting Ribbon (100% rayon, 100 yds each), 2 spools
• Crochet hook size G, or size to obtain gauge
• Safety pin
• 4½" plastic canvas round (optional)
• Approx 30 glass beads with large hole (optional)

Rnd 4 *Sc in next 2 sc, 2 sc in next sc; rep from * around—32 sc.
Rnd 5 Sc in each sc.
Rnd 6 *Sc in next 3 sc, 2 sc in next sc; rep from * around—40 sc.
Rnd 7 Rep rnd 5.
Rnd 8 *Sc in next 4 sc, 2 sc in next sc; rep from * around—48 sc.
Rnd 9 Rep rnd 5.
Rnd 10 Working in back lp of each st, *sc in next 5 sc, 2 sc in next sc; rep from * around—56 sts. Check gauge; circle should measure 5½" across. If circle is too small, work more rnds; if it is too large, remove rnds.

BODY

Mark first st of rnd with safety pin. Working through both lps of each sc, work rnds of sc until bag is about 7" from rnd 10.
Eyelet rnd Sl st in next st, ch 4 (counts as tr), tr in each sc around, end with sl st in top of beg ch 4. Ch 1, sc in same sp as join, sc in each tr around. Work 3 rnds sc. Work 1 rnd crab st (backward sc, from left to right). Fasten off.

FINISHING

Shoulder strap Ch 80". Sl st along edge of ch. Insert through eyelets on each side of bag on inside. Join with a sl st.
Drawstring closing Ch 30" and sl st along edge of ch. Weave in and out of eyelets and tie in bow in front of bag. Put bead on each end of cord, if desired, and knot.

DRAWSTRING BAG WITH BOBBLES

Work as for Basic Drawstring Bag through rnd 10.

BODY

Mark first st of rnd with safety pin.

Rnd 11 Working through both lp of sc for remainder of bag, sc in each sc around.

Rnds 12 to 13 Sc in each sc around.

Rnd 14 *Ch 7, sc in next 7 sc; rep from * around—8 bobbles.

Rnd 15 Keeping ch 7 lps to the front, sc in each sc around.

Rnds 16 to 17 Sc in each sc around.

Rnd 18 Sc in next 4 sc; *ch 7, sc in next 7 sc; rep from * ending ch 7, sc in next 3 sc.

Rnd 19 Rep rnd 15.

Rnds 20 to 21 Sc in each sc around.

Rnd 22 Rep rnd 14.

Cont in sc only until bag is 6" from rnd 10.

Next (bobble) rnd Sc in next sc, *ch 7, sc in next 2 sc; rep from * around, ending ch 7, sc in last sc. Keeping bobbles to the front, sc in each sc around. Work 2 rnds sc.

Work eyelet rnd and complete as for Basic Drawstring Bag.

DRAWSTRING BAG WITH BOBBLES, BEADS, AND FRINGE

Work as for Drawstring Bag with Bobbles until bag is 6" from rnd 10, join with a sl st in beg sc. Turn.

Add beads to fringe. Cut ribbon. String on approx 30 beads. Bead every other lp on first fringe row and every other lp on second fringe row. Alternate so beads do not lie on top of each other.

Fringe lps With WS facing, *sc in next 3 sc (wind ribbon around index finger of left hand once, insert hook in next st, bring hook under both strands of ribbon below lp on finger from front to back, and pull both strands at base of lp through sc, drop lp from finger, and hold down on RS of work, yo and draw through all 3 lps on hook = lp made); rep from * around; join with a sl st in beg sc; turn.

Rnd 2 Sc in each sc around, join to previous rnd.

Rnd 3 Sc in sc, *make lp in next sc, sc in next 3 sc; rep from * around, ending last rep, make lp in next sc, sc in next 2 sc, join, turn.

Sc in each sc around and around until bag is 7" from rnd 10. Work eyelet rnd and complete as for Basic Drawstring Bag.

"WEDDING CAKE" DRAWSTRING BAG (all fringed)

Work as for Basic Drawstring Bag through rnd 10.

BODY

Mark first st of rnd with safety pin. Working through both lps of each sc, work in sc for 2 rnds. *Work fringe lps as described in Drawstring Bag with Bobbles, Beads, and Fringe. Work 1 rnd sc, join. Work 1 rnd fringe lps, alternating them with row below. Work 4 rnds sc, join.* Rep from * to * until bag is approx 7" from rnd 10 of Basic Drawstring Bag. Work eyelet rnd and complete as for Basic Drawstring Bag.

FINISHING

Strap Ch approx 40". Sl st along edge of ch. Insert through eyelets on each side of bag on inside. Join one end of strap to the other with sl st. This will make a short wrist strap. For longer shoulder strap, see Basic Drawstring Bag.

Drawstring closing See Basic Drawstring Bag.

From left to right: drawstring bag with bobbles; drawstring bag with bobbles, beads, and fringe; and "wedding cake" drawstring bag.

Mini Evening "Shopping Bag"

Finished measurements
9" wide by 7" tall, from under the handle

Gauge In garter st, 16 sts and 16 rows = 4" using size 7 needles.

BAG (make 2 pieces)

With crochet hook, work 82 sc tightly around ring to cover (see page 5). Join with a sl st, ch 1, turn.
Rnd 1 Sc in each of next 28 sts.
With circular needle, pick up and k28 sts along last sc just worked. K1 row. Inc 1 st each end every other row 5 times—38 sts. Work in garter st (k every row) until piece measures 7" from top. Sl st tog on WS up to last inc.

FINISHING

BUTTON
Sew button on front of bag at top. Sew on tassel directly underneath button.

LOOP
Sl st Satin Cord to inside of opposite side of bag at bottom of handle. Ch approx 13 and attach with sl st to form lp for button. Weave in any loose ends.

MATERIALS
- Judi & Co.'s Satin Cord (144 yds each), 1 spool
- Crochet hook size D
- Circular needle size 7, or size to obtain gauge
- Straight needles size 7, if desired
- Two 4" diameter metal rings
- 1" diameter button
- 4" long rayon tassel

Crocheted Round Bag

Finished measurements (approximate)
8" diameter finished; 7" diameter unfinished
(size can be changed by adjusting the gauge)

BAG (make 2 pieces)

With larger hook, ch 3. Join with a sl st.
Rnd 1 Work 2 sc in back lp of each st—6 sts.
Rnd 2 Work 2 sc in back lp of each st—12 sts.
Rnd 3 Rep rnd 2—24 sts.
Rnd 4 *Work 1 sc in back lp of next 2 sts, work 2 sc in back lp of next st; rep from * around—32 sts.
Rnd 5 Sc in back lp of each sc. Fasten off.

FINISHING

Place front and back pieces tog, WS facing. Join with sc in back lp of each st, leaving 11 sts open at the top for opening and flap.

FLAP

Work sc across top of each of 11 sts left open along one side (work through both lps).

Work 3 rnds sc, then dec 1 st each end every rnd 3 times—5 sts. Do not cut ribbon.

BUTTON LP

With smaller hook, ch 8, sk 2 sc, join with a sl st to flap. Cut ribbon and weave in ends.

BACK HANDLE

Attach ribbon on one side of bag (just before start of flap). Ch 15, join to opposite side of bag (diagram A). Do not cut ribbon.

SHOULDER STRAP

Ch approx 30". Make lp as follows: sc in last 12 sts of ch and join with a sl st to form lp. Sl st all the way back across strap and bag handle. Ch approx 30" for opposite piece of strap. Make button as follows: Sc in last 9 sts from end of ch, join ninth st from end to third st from end with sl st. Push tail (3 sts) into center of lp to form button (diagram B). Sl st back to handle. Push crocheted button from one piece of strap through lp on opposite piece of strap. Length of strap can be adjusted by knotting around the lp. Knot can hang down as in diagram C. Fasten off and weave in ends.
Sew button on center of bag.
(Lining is suggested if bag is loosely crocheted.)

Diagram A   Diagram B

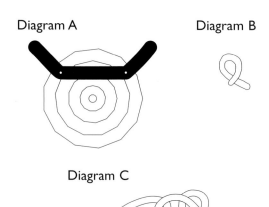

Diagram C

MATERIALS

- Judi & Co.'s ⅝" Double-Face Satin Acetate ribbon (100 yds each), 1 spool Red—or Judi & Co.'s ⅝" Matte ribbon (100 yds), 1 spool Ecru
- Crochet hooks sizes K and N
- One large button (approx 1¼" diameter)

Puff Bag

Crocheted version

Finished measurements
8" wide by 7" tall, including handle

BAG (make 2 pieces)
With F hook, attach yarn to first hole in handle, work sc in each hole—10 sts. Ch 1, turn. Cont in sc as follows:
Row 1 Inc in sc each st—20 sts. Ch 1, turn.
Row 2 Inc in sc every fifth st—24 sts. Ch 1, turn.
Row 3 Inc in sc every sixth st—28 sts. Ch 1, turn. Work even in sc until piece measures 4¾". Fasten off.

GUSSET
Ch 4, turn.
Row 1 Sc in second ch from hook and in each ch across—3 sts. Ch 1, turn.
Row 2 Sc in each sc. Ch 1, turn.
Rep row 2 until gusset measures approx 16". Do not cut cord.

MATERIALS (crocheted)
- Judi & Co.'s hand-dyed Satin Cord (144 yds each), 1 spool Peach Melba
- Crochet hook size F
- Two faux mother-of-pearl bag handles with holes (4½" by 2½")
- Yarn needle
- ¾" diameter mother-of-pearl button

FINISHING
Beg at first ch, whipstitch sides of gusset to sides of bag. Adjust gusset to fit. Fasten off.
Weave in all ends with yarn needle.

SHOULDER STRAP (optional)
Attach Satin Cord to top of side gusset. Ch for 45". Attach with sl st to other side of gusset. Sl st back to beg of ch. Fasten off. Bring strap through handle. This keeps handle straight up when using as shoulder bag.

BUTTON LP
Make lp and attach to inside center of one side of bag. Ch until piece is approx 3". Fold in half and sl st end to same spot as beg ch. Sew button on outside of bag opposite the lp.

Knitted version

Finished measurements
8" wide by 7" tall, including handle

BAG (make 2 pieces)
With F hook, attach yarn to first hole in handle. Sc in each hole—10 sts. Ch 1, turn.
Cont in sc as follows:
Row 1 Inc in sc each st—20 sts. Ch 1, turn.
Row 2 Inc in sc every fifth st—24 sts. Ch 1, turn.
Row 3 Sc in each st.
Row 4 Pick up and k24 sts with circular needle. Cont in garter st (k every row) as follows:
Row 5 Inc 1 st in every fifth st (to inc: pick up lp of st on needle—below the st—and put back on needle, k this st. This will give a much more even look)—28 sts.
Row 6 Inc 1 st in every sixth st—32 sts.

Work even in garter st until piece measures 4¾".
Bind off.

GUSSET

With knitting needle, cast on 6 sts. Work back and
forth in garter st for approx 16". Do not cut cord.

FINISHING

See Crocheted Puff Bag for instructions.

MATERIALS (knitted)

- Judi & Co.'s Cordé or Satin Cord (144
  yds each), 1 spool
- Crochet hook size F
- Two faux mother-of-pearl handles with
  holes (4½" by 2½")
- Yarn needle
- Circular needle size 5
- ⅝" diameter tortoise button

Knitted Cable Backpack

Finished measurements
12" tall, 11" wide, and 3½" deep

Gauge In seed st, 16 sts and 28 rows = 4" using larger size needles.

SEED ST

Row 1 (RS) *K1, p1; rep from * to end.
Row 2 K the p sts and p the k sts.
Rep row 2 for seed st.

HORSESHOE CABLE (over 14 sts)

Rows 1 and 3 (RS) P3, k8, p3.
Rows 2, 4, and 6 K3, p8, k3.
Row 5 P3, sl next 2 sts to cn and hold to *back* of work, k2, k2 from cn, sl next 2 sts to cn, and hold to *front* of work, k2, k2 sts from cn, p3.
Rep rows 1 to 6 for horseshoe cable.

BAG

With larger needles, cast on 104 sts.

BEG PATS

Row 1 (RS) Work 6 sts seed st [14 sts horseshoe cable, 12 sts seed st] 3 times, 14 sts

horseshoe cable, 6 sts seed st. Cont in pats as established until piece measures 11". End with a WS row.

EYELET ROW

Work first 20 sts in seed st and sl to stitch holder, work next 64 sts in seed st, work rem 20 sts in seed and sl to another holder. Cut Soutache. Join Soutache and work on center 64 sts in seed st as follows:
Row 1 [Work 3 sts, k2 tog, yo] 5 times, work next 14 sts (no eyelets), [k2 tog, yo, work 3 sts] 5 times. Work seed st on next row, working each yo as a st. Work 4 rows even in seed st. Bind off loosely on next row.

FLAP

Whipstitch center back seam. Sl 40 sts from stitch holders to smaller needles. Work in seed st, dec 8 sts evenly on first row—32 sts. Cont on these sts in seed st for 3". Dec 1 st each end every other row 9 times—14 sts. Bind off loosely.

BASE

With smaller needles, cast on 7 sts. Work in seed st, inc 1 st each end every other row 4 times—15 sts. Cont on 15 sts until piece measures 9". Dec 1 st each end every other row 4 times—7 sts. Bind off.

STRAPS (make 2)

With smaller needles, cast on 8 sts. Work in seed st for 24". Bind off. Whipstitch straps at top inside cable pat on back (seed st area). Attach bottom of straps to cable pat near base of bag.

DRAWSTRING CORD

With size F hook, ch for 35". Make lp with

Soutache on inside center back of bag on same level as eyelets. This will hold the cord straight as it passes on the inside back of bag from point E to point F. Fasten off and cut. Beg weaving through eyelets at point A on right front of bag (follow the diagram below). Knot ends of drawstring.

MAGNETIC SNAPS

Crocheted pieces With size F hook, ch 5. Sc in second ch from hook and in each ch across. Ch 1, turn—4 sts.

Next row Sc in each sc across. Ch 1, turn. Rep last row until piece measures 1".

Place one half of the magnetic snap in the crocheted piece by inserting the prongs through the fabric and the metal washer. Bend prongs over washer. Position crocheted piece on inside flap of bag and sew in place with Soutache. Line up other half of snap on corresponding area of front of bag and assemble as before.

Pattern for Inserting Drawstring

	SIDE				FRONT			SIDE			
	I	I	I	I	I		I	I	I	I	I
						seed						
out F	in G	out H	in I	out J		st	in A	out B	in C	out D	in E

Luminesse Drawstring Bag

Finished measurements
9" tall, 7" wide, and 5" deep

PAT ST

Row 1 (RS) *K next st, wrapping yarn twice around needle; rep from * to end.
Row 2 *K next st, letting extra wrap drop; rep from * to end.

BAG

Beg at top of bag, with size 9 needles, cast on 60 sts. Work 8 rows in garter st (k every row).
Eyelet row (RS) K1 *yarn forward, k2 tog; rep from *, end k1.

BODY

K next row. Work 2 rows pat st. Work 2 rows garter st. Work 2 rows pat st. [Work in St st (k on RS, p on WS) for 4 rows, work in garter st for 4 rows] 3 times.

MATERIALS

- Judi & Co.'s Luminesse ¼" Rayon Ribbon (100% rayon, 100 yds each), 2 skeins Wild Iris
- Straight knitting needles size 9, or size to obtain gauge
- 4½" diameter plastic canvas
- Two large-hole glass beads
- Crochet hook size F

SHAPE BASE

Next row (RS) [K2 tog, k8] 6 times—54 sts.
P1 row.
Next row (RS) [K2 tog, k7] 6 times—48 sts.
P1 row.
Cont in this way to dec 6 sts every other row until 6 sts rem. Cut yarn and thread through rem sts.

FINISHING

Sew seam.

DRAWSTRING

Ch approx 26". Thread through every other opening in eyelet row. Thread ch through glass beads and knot ends.

SHOULDER STRAP

Attach ribbon with sl st to the side of top of bag. Ch approx 32" or desired length. Attach to opposite side of top with sl st. Weave in all ends.

STEAMING

Steam bag lightly. Steam bottom so that it stays flat. Insert plastic round in bottom.
(Knitted bag should be lined to pat st 1 or up to eyelets.)

STRAPS AND DRAWSTRING TOGETHER
(alternate suggestion)

You can also work 2 long chains and thread them through the eyelets in opposite directions. Put on beads and then tie an overhand knot at the ends. This would eliminate the separate drawstring.

Evening Bag

Finished measurements
6½" wide by 5½" tall, with 4" flap

BODY

With size G hook, ch 50. Hdc in third ch from hook, then in each ch across. Cont in hdc, working ch 2, turn at end of every row (counts as 1 hdc), until piece measures 5½" from beg. Cut ribbon. Join sides with seam in center back using yarn needle.

BASE

With size G hook, ch 15. Work hdc in each ch across. On next row, inc 1 st each side (work 2 hdc in same st)—17 hdc. Work 1 row even. Then dec 1 st each end—15 hdc. Work 1 row even. Cut ribbon.
Sew base to bottom of bag.

FLAP

Sc in 14 sts along center back. Ch 2, turn. Work hdc until flap measures 4". Fasten off. Work 1 row sc around flap.

MAGNETIC SNAPS

Make crocheted piece for inside of flap. With size G hook, ch 5. Sc in second ch from hook and each ch across. Ch 1, turn—4 sts. Next row: Sc in each sc. Ch 1, turn. Rep last row until piece measures 1" long. Place one half of magnetic snap in cro-cheted piece by inserting the prongs through the fabric and the metal washer. Bend prongs over washer. Position crocheted piece on inside of flap and sew in place with same material as bag. Line up other half of snap on body of bag to provide easy closing of the flap and assemble as before.

SHOULDER STRAP

Pull up lp on one side of top of body of bag for strap. Ch 44", or length desired, and attach to opposite side. Work sl st in each ch across. Attach to opposite end. Cut ribbon and weave in ends. Attach rhinestone button on top of lower edge of flap.

STEAMING

Steam finished bag lightly and pull it into shape. Lay flat to dry. Be sure to use pressing cloth over bag.

MATERIALS
- Judi & Co.'s ½" Rayon Knitting Ribbon (100% rayon, 100 yds each), 2 spools
- Crochet hook size G
- Yarn needle
- ¾" diameter magnetic snap
- ½" diameter rhinestone button

Evening bag (left) and ribbon backpack.

Ribbon Backpack

Finished measurements
6½" wide by 7½" tall, with 4" flap (see photo on page 81)

BODY

With size G hook, ch 50. Hdc in third ch from hook, then in each ch across. Cont in hdc, working ch 2, turn at end of every row (counts as 1 hdc) until piece measures 7½" from beg. Cut ribbon. Join sides with seam in center of back using yarn needle.

BASE

With size G hook, ch 15. Work hdc in each ch across. On next row inc 1 st each side (work 2 hdc in same st)—17 hdc. Work 1 row even. Then dec 1 st each end on next row—15 hdc. Work 1 row even. Cut ribbon.
Sew base to bottom of bag.

FLAP

Sc in 14 sts along center back. Ch 2, turn. Work hdc until flap measures 4". Fasten off. Work 1 row sc around flap.

STRAP

Ch 40". Work sc in each ch across. Cut ribbon.

ATTACH STRAP TO BAG

Hold bag with back facing. Beg at fourth row from bottom on back and approx 1" in from RS, thread end of strap through to inside of bag and knot strap. Bring other end of strap through top of RS of back about 1" over to left of bottom part of strap and directly under flap. Thread through to inside of bag. Turn bag so that front is facing. Thread through side and front of bag until reach-

ing opposite side back. Go through back under the flap. Turn bag so that back is facing. Bring strap through back and down the left side so that strap lines up with strap on RS. Bring strap through back of bag to inside of bag and knot strap.

MAGNETIC SNAPS

Follow directions on page 80. Attach frog.

STEAMING

Steam finished bag lightly and pull it into shape. Lay flat to dry. Be sure to use pressing cloth over bag.

MATERIALS

- Judi & Co.'s Rayon ½" Knitting Ribbon (100% rayon, 100 yds each), 2 spools
- Crochet hook size G
- Yarn needle
- ¾" diameter magnetic snap
- Frog with tassel

Attaching straps

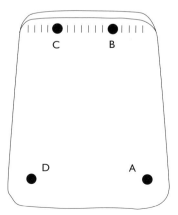

Flapper Drawstring Bag

Finished measurements
9" tall and 7½" wide (see photo on page 84)

Gauge In garter st, 16 sts and 16 rows = 4" using size 7 needles.

WAVE ST (multiple of 12 sts plus 1)
Rows 1 to 4 K.
Rows 5, 7, 9, and 11 (RS) K1, *[k2 tog] twice, [yo, k1] 3 times, yo, [ssk] twice, k1; rep from * to end.
Rows 6, 8, 10, and 12 P.

BAG (make 2 pieces)
With size 7 needles, cast on 37 sts. Work rows 1 to 12 of wave pat.
Row 13 (RS) K, dec 5 sts evenly across—32 sts. Work in garter st until piece measures 7½" from bottom of scallop, end with a WS row.
Eyelet row (RS) K1 *k2 tog, yo; rep from *, end k1. K1 row. Work 1" in garter st. Bind off.

MATERIALS
- Judi & Co's Satin Cord (144 yds each), 1 skein hand-dyed "Peacock"
- Straight knitting needles size 7, or size to obtain gauge
- Fray Check
- Crochet hook size F
- ½ yd #9 (1½") satin or grosgrain ribbon in MC or CC, or ¼ yd lining fabric to match
- 15 to 20 assorted glass pony and donut beads (optional)

FINISHING

OPTIONAL
If you don't want to line your bag fully, cut ribbon in half and pin to bottom of WS of bag over the open work. Fold in about ½" of ends of ribbon. Cut off excess ribbon, then whipstitch ribbon to bag, making sure to keep the ribbon loose.

ATTACH SIDES
With RS facing, whipstitch sides tog. At the bottom, turn RS out and whipstitch bottom tog. Weave in all ends (leave Satin Cord ends long).

CORDS (make 2)
Ch 40" or length desired. Weave through eyelets starting at *opposite sides* of bag (see diagram A). Attach back cords tog with sl st and knot ends, leaving a few inches. Rep same with front cords. String a few beads on end of each cord. Tie knot and cut to desired length. Put Fray Check on ends (see diagram B).

Diagram A

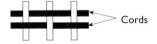

Diagram B (from top of bag, looking down)

Flapper drawstring bag (left) and flapper wrist bag.

TRIM

Cut 2 pieces of Satin Cord approx 10" long.
Thread through bag in center under drawstring
row. Leave at uneven lengths and tie each tog.

Thread a few glass beads on each cord, tying a
knot to hold them in place. Put a dab of Fray
Check on Satin Cord ends to prevent fraying.

Flapper Wrist Bag

Finished measurements
9½" tall and 7½" wide

Gauge In garter st, 16 sts and 16 rows = 4" using size 7 needles.

WAVE ST (multiple of 12 sts plus 1)
Rows 1 to 4 K.
Rows 5, 7, 9, and 11 (RS) K1, *[k2 tog] twice, [yo, k1] 3 times, yo, [ssk] twice, k1; rep from * to end.
Rows 6, 8, 10, and 12 P.

BAG (make 2 pieces)
With size 7 needles, cast on 37 sts. Work rows 1 to 12 of wave pat.
Row 13 (RS) K, dec 5 sts evenly across—32 sts. Work in garter st (k every row) until piece measures 6" from bottom of scallop, end with RS row. On next (WS) row, k2 tog across row—16 sts. Beg and end with k1, work in p2, k2 rib for 4". Bind off in pat or put on stitch holder for three-needle bind-off.

FINISHING
Sew handle tog or do three-needle bind-off.

OPTIONAL
If you don't want to line your bag fully, cut ribbon in half and pin to bottom of WS of bag over the open work. Fold in about ½" of ends of ribbon. Cut off excess ribbon and then whipstitch ribbon to bag, making sure to keep the ribbon loose.

ATTACH SIDES
With RS facing, whipstitch sides tog. At the bottom, turn RS out and whipstitch bottom tog. Weave in all ends. (Leave Satin Cord ends long.)

SEW BUTTON
Sew button on bag just under rib pat handle. Cut 2 pieces of Satin Cord approx 10" long. Thread through bag under button. Leave at uneven lengths and tie each tog. Thread a few glass beads on each cord, tying a knot to hold them in place. Put dab of Fray Check on Satin Cord ends to prevent fraying.

MATERIALS
- Judi & Co's Satin Cord (144 yds each), 1 spool Ivory
- Straight knitting needles size 7, or size to obtain gauge
- Fray Check
- ½ yd #9 (1½") satin or grosgrain ribbon in MC or CC, or ¼ yd lining fabric to match
- 1" diameter shell button (optional)
- 12 to 15 assorted glass pony and donut beads (optional)

Hobo Bags

Striped version

Finished measurements
24" tall and 11" wide, including handle

Gauge In garter st, 18 sts and 32 rows = 4" using size 7 needles.

Note When changing colors for the stripe pats, leave a long enough piece of that color to use when sewing bag tog.

STRAPS (make 2)

With size 7 needles, cast on 6 sts. Work in garter st (k every row) for 7". Inc 1 st each end every other row until 48 sts or approx 11" across. Join 2

pieces tog—96 sts—and work with one skein. Work even in garter st until piece measures approx 9¾", end with a WS row. Dec 6 sts evenly across next k row. P1 row. Cont in St st (k on RS, p on WS) and work as follows:

ROUNDED BAG BOTTOM

Row 1 [K8, k2 tog] 9 times, k6—87 sts.
Row 2 and all WS rows P.
Row 3 [K7, k2 tog] 9 times, k6—78 sts.
Cont in this way to dec 9 sts every other row until there are 15 sts.
Leaving about an 18" length, cut raffia. Using a yarn needle, weave through rem sts. Fasten off.

FINISHING

Whipstitch center seams tog. (If bag has stripes, make sure to match exactly and sew tog with matching color.) With crochet hook and MC, work 1 row sc around straps.

BAG TIES

Attach raffia (MC) to center of one side of bag opening. Ch approx 11". Sl st back along one side of ch and fasten off. Tie should measure approx 10". Rep on opposite side of bag for closing. Pull crocheted tie through hole of bead. Knot end.

MAGNETIC SNAPS (make 2)

Make crocheted pieces. With size F hook, ch 5. Sc in second chain from hook and each ch across. Ch 1, turn—4 sts. Next row: Sc in each sc. Ch 1, turn. Rep last row until piece is 1" long. Place half of magnetic snap in crocheted piece by inserting the prongs through the fabric and metal washer. Bend prongs over washer. Position crocheted piece on inside of bag and sew in place with same material

Basic bag

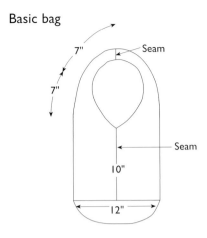

Stripe Pattern I

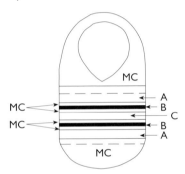

Mini raffia knit purse and hobo bags (left to right: stripe pats II, III, and I).

as bag. Line up other half of snap on other side of bag and assemble as before.

STEAMING

Finished bag must be steamed lightly and pulled into shape. Lay flat to dry. Be sure to use pressing cloth over bag.

LINING (optional)

If desired, line only up to the separation for the straps.

STRIPE PAT I

Follow directions for basic bag body until 96 sts. Work 1 more row in MC. Change to stripe pat.

Starting from top 8 rows MC, 10 rows A, 4 rows MC, 4 rows B, 4 rows MC, 10 rows C, 4 rows MC, 4 rows B, 4 rows MC, 10 rows A, 8

rows MC. With MC, dec for bottom of bag and finish following basic bag directions.

STRIPE PAT II

Follow directions for basic bag body until 96 sts. **Optional** Work 10 rows of C when first starting the straps (as in photo). It looks pretty but makes it a little more difficult to hide the ends. Change to MC and cont to work straps.

Starting from top 4 rows B, 2 rows C, 8 rows A, 2 rows MC, 2 rows C, 4 rows B, 8 rows C, 2 rows MC, 2 rows C, 8 rows A, 4 rows B, 2 rows MC, 8 rows C, 2 rows MC, 2 rows C, 8 rows MC. With MC, dec for bottom of bag and finish following basic bag directions.

STRIPE PAT III

Follow directions for basic bag body until 96 sts.

Starting from top 10 rows B, 2 rows A, 4 rows C, 2 rows A, 4 rows B, 2 rows MC, 4 rows C, 10 rows MC, 4 rows B, 2 rows A, 4 rows C, 2 rows A, 10 rows B, 2 rows MC, 2 rows C, 6 rows MC. Dec for bottom of bag and finish following basic bag directions.

Slipstitch version

Finished measurements
24" tall and 11" wide, including handle

Gauge
In sl st pat, 18 sts and 32 rows = 4" using size 7 needles.

SL ST PAT (multiple of 4 sts plus 3)
Row 1 (RS) *K3, sl 1; rep from *, end k3.
Row 2 P.
Rep rows 1 and 2 for sl st pat.

STRAPS (make 2)
With size 7 needles, cast on 7 sts. Work in sl st pat for 7". Inc 1 st each end (working inc sts into sl st pat) every other row until 51 sts or approx 11" across. Join 2 pieces tog—102 sts and work with one skein. Work even in sl st pat until piece measures approx 9¾", end with a WS row. Dec 2 sts evenly across next row—100 sts. P1 row. Cont in St st (k on RS, p on WS) and work as follows:

MATERIALS (slipstitch)
- Judi & Co.'s Rayon Raffia (72 yds each), 5 skeins
- Straight knitting needles size 7, or size to obtain gauge
- Crochet hook size F
- Yarn needle
- Two large-hole beads or "fruit drops"
- ¾" diameter magnetic snap

ROUNDED BAG BOTTOM
Row 1 [K8, k2 tog] 10 times—90 sts.
Row 2 and all WS rows P.
Row 3 [K7, k2 tog] 10 times—80 sts.
Cont in this way to dec 10 sts every other row until there are 10 sts. Leaving about an 18" length, cut raffia. Using yarn needle, weave through rem sts. Fasten off.

FINISHING
Whipstitch center seam tog. With crochet hook, work 1 row sc around straps.

BAG TIES
Attach raffia to center of one side of bag opening. Ch approx 11". Sl st back along 1 side of ch and fasten off. Tie should measure approx 10". Rep on opposite side of bag for closing. Pull crocheted tie through hole of bead. Knot end.

MAGNETIC SNAPS (make 2)
Make crocheted pieces. With size F hook, ch 5. Sc in second ch from hook and each ch across. Ch 1, turn—4 sts. Next row: Sc in each sc. Ch 1, turn. Rep last row until piece is 1" long. Place one half of magnetic snap in crocheted piece by inserting the prongs through the fabric and the metal washer. Bend prongs over washer. Position crocheted piece on inside of bag and sew in place with same material as bag. Line up the other half of the snap on other side of bag and assemble as before.

STEAMING
Finished bag must be steamed lightly and pulled into shape. Lay flat to dry. Be sure to use a pressing cloth over the bag.

LINING (optional)
If desired, line only up to the separation for the straps.

Mini Raffia Knit Purse

Finished measurements
5" wide by 4" tall, with 2" flap

Gauge In garter st, 18 sts and 32 rows = 4" using size 7 needles.

Note Purse can be worked in random stripes or blocks of color. Blanket st looks best in CC.

PURSE

With size 7 needles, cast on 23 sts. Work in garter st (k every row) for 9½".

WORK BUTTONHOLE

K10, bind off 3 sts, work to end. On next row, k9, and inc by working into front and back of this st, cast on 2 more sts and k10. K1 more row and bind off loosely.

FINISHING

Steam piece lightly into shape. When dry, fold bottom up 4". Fold 2" of flap over. Either work sc around sides and flap of bag or st tog using blanket st as in drawing at right.
Sew button to inside front of bag to line up with buttonhole.

MATERIALS

- Judi & Co.'s Rayon Raffia, leftover of one or more colors
- Straight knitting needles size 7, or size to obtain gauge
- One ¾" diameter plastic or wooden button

Blanket stitch

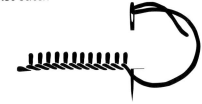

Victorian Envelope Bag

Finished measurements
8" wide by 10" tall when unfolded (8" by 6" folded)

Gauge In double moss st, 16 sts and 26 rows = 4" using size 9 needles.

DOUBLE MOSS ST

Row 1 (RS) *K2, p2; rep from * to end.
Rows 2 and 4 K the k sts and p the p sts.
Row 3 *P2, k2*; rep from * to end.
Rep rows 1 to 4 for double moss st.

BACK

Beg at the lower edge, cast on 32 sts. Work in double moss st for 7½", ending with either row 1 or row 3.
Flap Dec 1 st at beg of every row 12 times—20 sts. Bind off in pat.

FRONT

Work as for back until piece measures 5½". Bind off in pat.

FINISHING

Steam pieces. Sew 3 sides tog with a whipstitch, using ribbon and yarn needle. Sew hook-and-loop circle to inside flap of bag and corresponding part of bag with sewing needle and thread. Fold bag to measure about 6".
Steam bag again. Sew lining to inside of bag. Cut length of ribbon 20" and apply spray starch. Make a bow with the ribbon. Make another bow with the fused pearls and sew both bows onto bag flap near edge. Sew silk flowers on top of ribbon and pearls.

MATERIALS

- Judi & Co's ½" Rayon Ribbon (100% rayon, 100 yds each), 2 spools
- Straight knitting needles size 9, or size to obtain gauge
- One small hook-and-loop circle
- Yarn needle
- Sewing needle with matching thread
- Small bunch of silk roses measuring approx 2" in diameter
- 20" piece of small fused pearls
- Lining fabric measuring approx 12" by 18"
- Spray starch

Round Bridal Bag

Finished measurements

Approx 7" in diameter (size can be changed by adjusting the gauge)

BAG (make 2 pieces)

With larger hook, ch 3. Join with sl st.

Rnd 1 Work 2 sc in back lp of each st—6 sts.

Rnd 2 Work 2 sc in back lp of each st—12 sts.

Rnd 3 Rep row 2—24 sts.

Rnd 4 *Work 1 sc in back lp of next 2 sts, work 2 sc in back lp of next st; rep from * to end—32 sts.

Rnd 5 Sc in back lp of each st. Fasten off and weave in all ends (approx 5½" in diameter).

FINISHING

Place front and back pieces tog with WS facing. Join with sc in back lp of each st, leaving 11 sts open at the top for opening and flap.

MATERIALS

- Judi & Co.'s ⅝" double-face woven Satin Acetate ribbon (approx 50 yds)
- Crochet hooks sizes K and N
- 1½" to 2" diameter button
- 4" tassel (optional)
- Lining fabric (optional)

FLAP

Work sc across top of each of 11 sts left open along one side (work through both lps).
Work 3 rows even, then dec 1 st each end every row 3 times—5 sts. Do not cut ribbon.

BUTTON LP

With smaller hook, ch 8. Sk 2 sc on bag, attach with sl st to flap. Cut ribbon and weave in ends.

SHOULDER STRAP

Attach ribbon to one side of bag with a sl st. Ch 40" or desired length. Attach to opposite side with sl st. Fasten off and weave in all ends.

BUTTON

Sew button on center of bag. Attach tassel to buttonhole lp by inserting lp of tassel through the front of buttonhole lp and sew it in the back.

LINING

Lining is suggested if bag is crocheted loosely.

Patchwork Drawstring Bag

Finished measurements
9" wide by 10" tall, with 2" gusset.

GRANNY SQUARE (make 8)

Foundation ch rnd With A, ch 6, join with a sl st to form a ring.

Rnd 1 Ch 3 (counts as 1 dc), in ring work: 2 dc, ch 3, [3 dc, ch 3] 3 times, join with a sl st.

Rnd 2 With B, sl st to first sp, (ch 3, 2 dc, ch 3, 3 dc) into first ch-3 sp, (ch 1, 3 dc, ch 3, 3 dc) into each corner; rep from *, ending ch 1, join with a sl st.

Rnd 3 With B, sl st to first sp, (ch 2, 2 dc, ch 3, 3 dc) into first ch-3 sp, *ch 1, 3 dc into ch-1 sp, (ch 1, 3 dc, ch 3, 3 dc) into next corner; rep from *, end ch 1, join with a sl st. Fasten off.

Rnd 4 With MC, rep rnd 3, adding an extra 3 dc on each side.

Weave in all ends.

FINISHING

Sl st 4 squares tog for front. Rep for back.

MATERIALS

- Judi & Co's Satin Cord (144 yds each), 1 spool Black (MC), 1 spool Eggshell (A), and 1 spool Brown (B)
- Crochet hook size G
- Yarn needle
- Two ¾" Faux Tortoise donuts or large hole beads
- Lining fabric

GUSSET

Row 1 With MC, ch 7.

Row 2 Sc in second ch from hook, then in each ch across, ch 1, turn.

Row 3 Sc in each sc, ch 1, turn.

Rep row 3 until piece measures approx 28" and fits around 3 sides of bag. Beg whipstitching gusset to one side of bag, starting with cast-on edge first. Adjustments can be made later to length of gusset. Attach gusset in this manner to other side of bag.

Pinch in gusset at top edges to form an inverted pleat. Sew in place with MC. Starting at one side of gusset, work 2 rows sc around top of bag. Work 1 row crab st. (Backwards crochet, from left to right.)

STRAP

Attach Satin Cord to top of one side of gusset and sc 6 sts for strap, ch 1, turn. Strap should be 1¼" wide. Work in sc until strap measures 30". Attach to other side of gusset with sl sts.

DRAWSTRING

Ch approx 35". Sl st across ch and fasten off. Thread drawstring through holes of top granny squares in back and front of bag as in the right drawing on the facing page. Push ends of cord through donuts and fold over. Weave in all ends and sew down with sewing thread.

LINING

Lining is required for this bag (see page 5).

Granny square

Approximate size: 4¼" by 4¼"

Right half of front of bag

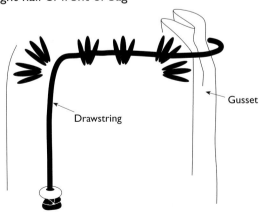

Drawstring

Gusset

Chapter 3

ACCESSORIES

*A*ccessories such as hats, scarves, and shawls are perfect complements to any wardrobe. The accessories in this chapter are deceivingly simple and most can be worked by first-time knitters and crocheters because you don't have to worry about shaping. What's more, the projects are easily adaptable to any color ribbon you choose.

MATERIALS

- Judi & Co's Rayon Satin Cord (144 yds each), 2 spools Ivory (MC) (there will be enough left over in MC to make flower and leaves all in MC, if desired); 20 yds Shocking Pink (A); 5 yds Apple Green (B)
- Crochet hook size H, or size to obtain gauge
- Yarn needle
- Fray Check
- Safety pins

Flapper Hat

Size One size fits most.

Gauge In hdc, 4 hdc = 1"; 7 rows = 2" using size H crochet hook.

Notes Always leave long ends in Satin Cord and make sure to weave-in in several places. Ends that are too short can fray. Fray Check is recommended on those ends to prevent unraveling. When making the hat, mark each round with a safety pin.

HAT

Ch 4, join with a sl st to form a ring.
Rnd 1 Work 8 hdc in ring.
Rnd 2 Work 2 hdc in each st around—16 hdc.
Rnd 3 Work 2 hdc in each st around—32 hdc.
Rnd 4 *Work 1 hdc in each of next 4 sts, 2 hdc in next st; rep from * around.
Rep rnd 4 until piece measures approx 6" to 6½" in diameter (or across). Work 1 rnd even in hdc in back lp of st. Work next rnd in both lps of st and cont until piece measures approx 3½" from marked rnd.
Next rnd Dc in each st around. This is the openwork rnd for tie.

BRIM

Rnd 1 *Hdc in each of next 3 sts, 2 hdc in next st; rep from * around.
Rnd 2 Hdc in each st. Rep rnd 2 four more times. Fasten off.

CABBAGE ROSE

Ch 4, join with a sl st to form a ring.
Rnd 1 Ch 1, 10 sc in ring, join with a sl st to beg ch 1.
Rnd 2 Ch 2, sk next sc, *sl st in next sc, ch 2, sk next sc; rep from * around, ending with sl st in first sc—5 ch-2 lps.
Rnd 3 (Sl st, ch 2, 4 dc, ch 2, sl st) in each ch-2 sp—5 petals.
Rnd 4 Working behind petals, *sl st in next skipped sc on rnd 2, ch 3; rep from * around, join with sl st in first st—5 ch-3 lps.
Rnd 5 (Sl st, ch 2, 7 dc, ch 2, sl st) in each ch-3 sp around—5 petals.
Rnd 6 Working behind petals, *sc around ch lp of rnd 4 and between center 2 dc on next petal, ch 4; rep from * around, join with a sl st in first sc—5 ch-4 lps.
Rnd 7 (Sl st, ch 2, 10 dc, ch 2, sl st) in each ch-4 sp around—5 petals. Fasten off.

LEAVES (make 2)

Leaving an end of about 5", ch 8. Sc in second ch from hook, hdc, 3dc, hdc, sc, ch 4 for stem. Pull through loop and end.

FINISHING

With Satin Cord, ch approx 28" to make the tie. Fasten off. Thread tie through dc rnd, try on for fit, and tie a knot to adjust size.
With Satin Cord and yarn needle, sew flower to left side of hat above knot.
Attach leaves to left and right of flower with Satin Cord.

Knit Evening Shawl

Finished measurements
Approx 23" by 56" (including points at both ends)

Notes Always k2 sts at beg and end of each p row when working any St st section to keep edges from curling.
Leave long ends of ribbon (around 4" to 5") to be woven in or sewn when finishing.
Gauge is not critical. Length can be changed by adding more rows St st in pat I or adding I section more of pats I and II. (Materials will change.)

PAT ST I

Rows I and 2 With B, k. (Do not cut B. Carry to row 5.)
Row 3 With A, k.
Row 4 With A, k2, p to last 2 sts, k2.
Rows 5 and 6 With B and C tog, k.
Row 7 Drop C and use B only as follows: *k1, wrapping yarn twice around needle, k1*; rep from * to end.
Row 8 *K1, dropping extra wraps, k1*; rep from * to end.
Rows 9 and 10 With B and C tog, k. (Do not cut B.)
Row 11 With A, k.
Row 12 With A, p.
Rows 13 and 14 With B, k.

PAT ST II

Rows I to 12 With A, work in St st.
Attach C and work with A on rows 13 and 14.
Rows 13 and 14 K. (Prestrung small crystal beads on a fine thread can be knitted in on these rows instead of Fur.)
Rows 15 to 26 With A, work in St st.

SHAWL
POINTS
Make separately and then work together on same needle. K all rows.
With A, cast on 2 sts.
Row I K2.
Row 2 Inc I st each end—4 sts.
Row 3 K.
Cont in this way to inc I st each end every other row until there are 10 sts. Cut ribbon, leaving long end on all but last point. Use same needle to cast on for each point so that all points end upon same needle. Work total of 7 points. Cont to work on all 70 sts as follows: With A, work 2 rows garter st, 4 rows St st (k on RS, p on WS).
*Work 14 rows pat st 1, 26 rows pat st 2. Rep from * (40 rows) 4 times more. Work 14 rows pat st I once more. There are 6 sections of pat st I and 5 sections of pat st II. With A, work 4 rows St st, 2 rows garter st.

END POINTS
Divide into 7 sections (10 sts each). Work each point separately, attaching ribbon before working new point.
Row I K2 tog, k6, k2 tog—8 sts.
Row 2 K.
Cont in this way to dec 2 sts every other row until there are 2 sts.
Last row K2 tog.
Cut ribbon, leaving about 8" length. Join ribbon. Work on next 10 sts in same way.

FINISHING

Attach large glass beads to ribbon at bottom of point. Weave ribbon through to back. Weave in all ends. Steam lightly into shape using a pressing cloth. A row of sc can be worked around each pat II section if desired.

MATERIALS

- Judi & Co.'s Charmeuse Rayon Ribbon (70 yds each), 7 spools Black or Ecru (A)
- Judi & Co.'s Dazzle ¼" Rayon Ribbon (100% rayon, 100 yds each), 2 spools Black or Ecru (B)
- Baruffa Fur Deluxe, 1 ball Black or White (C)
- Straight knitting needles size 10, or size to obtain gauge
- 14 large beads, glass donuts, or teardrop pearls

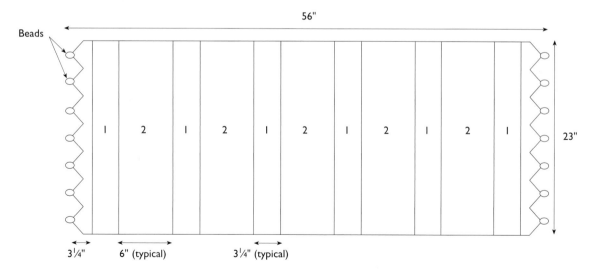

Krinkle Cowl with Tassel

Finished measurements
Approx 10" by 32"

Gauge In double moss st, 13 sts = 4" using size 10½ needles.

Note This is an easy piece for beginner knitters who don't want to do shaping.

DOUBLE MOSS ST (multiple of 4 sts)

Row 1 (RS) *K2, p2*, rep from * to end.
Row 2 K the k sts and p the p sts.
Row 3 *P2, k2*, rep from * to end.
Row 4 Rep row 2.
Rep rows 1 to 4 for double moss st.

COWL

With size 10½ needles, cast on 32 sts. Work in double moss st for approx 32". Bind off loosely.

FINISHING

Steam finished piece lightly. Turn one end once, creating a twist in the piece, as in diagram A. Weave the two ends together.

TASSEL (optional)

Wrap ribbon loosely around a 4½" by 4½" piece of cardboard (diagram B).
Thread a strand of ribbon through the top and tie firmly with a square knot, leaving a long enough end for sewing to cowl.
Cut strands at bottom.
Hide knot and short end left from tying it under folded strands.
Wrap a length of ribbon several times around top of lp (folded end) about 1" down from the top. Tie tightly and thread through tassel so that ends are hidden.
Trim ends.
Attach tassel to one edge of cowl approx 12" from seam (diagram C).

MATERIALS

- Tahki Imports Ltd. hand-dyed Rayon Krinkle Ribbon (72 yds each), 3 skeins color 71
- Straight knitting needles size 10½, or size to obtain gauge
- Yarn needle

Diagram A

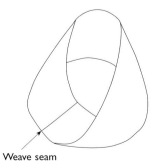

Weave seam

Diagram B

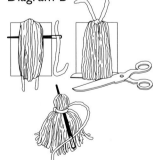

Diagram C

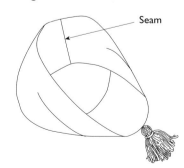

Seam

Resources

Most of the materials used in this book are available from the author.

Judi & Co.
18 Gallatin Dr.
Dix Hills, NY 11746
(516) 499-8480

BUTTONS
These companies can refer you to yarn shops that carry beautiful and unusual buttons.

Blue Moon Button Art
406 Mission St.
Santa Cruz, CA 95060
(408) 457-6333   Fax: (408) 457-6324

Bonnie Maresh Glass Buttons
P.O. Box 3037
Waquoit, MA 02536
(508) 548-6215   Fax: (508) 540-4616

buttons, etc.
2 Heitz Pl.
Hicksville, NY 11801
(800) 237-0613   Fax: (516) 931-4436

Renaissance Buttons
P.O. Box 130
Oregon House, CA 95962
(916) 692-1663   Fax: (916) 692-1090

Sew Buttons, Inc.
389 Fifth Ave., Room 1015
New York, NY 10016
(212) 696-9252   Fax: (212) 696-9512

GLASS BEADS
The following mail-order companies have catalogs available.

Bead Warehouse
4 Meadowlake Dr.
Mendon, VT 05701
(802) 775-3082

Beadbox
10135 E. Via Linda, Suite C116
Scottsdale, AZ 85258
(800) BEADBOX   (602) 451-4563
e-mail: beadbox@worldnet.att.net
www.beadbox.com

Shipwreck Beads
2727 Westmoor Ct. S.W.
Olympia, WA 98502
(360) 754-2323
www.shipwreck.com

YARNS AND RIBBON
Most of the yarn companies listed here offer one or two ribbon-type yarns. Write for information on stores that carry their products in your area.

Great Adirondack Yarn Co.
950 County Hwy. 126
Amsterdam, NY 12010

JCA
35 Scales Ln.
Townsend, MA 01469

Plymouth Yarn Co.
P.O. Box 28
Bristol, PA 19007

Tahki Yarns
11 Graphic Pl.
Moonachie, NJ 07074

Stacy Charles Collection
1061 Manhattan Ave.
Brooklyn, NY 11222

Trendsetter Yarns
16742 Stagg St., Unit 104
Van Nuys, CA 91406

The following mail-order companies
offer a wide variety of rayon ribbon.

Colorful Stitches
48 Main St.
Lenox, MA 01240
(800) 413-6111   (413) 637-8206

Crafty Lady
15401 Hall Rd.
Macomb, MI 48044
(800) 455-9276   (810) 566-8008

Garden City Stitches
725 Franklin Ave.
Garden City, NY 11530
(516) 739-5648   Fax: (516) 739-3757

Great Yarns
1208 Ridge Rd.
Raleigh, NC 27607
(800) 810-0045   (919) 832-3599

La Knitterie Parisienne
12642 Ventura Blvd.
Studio City, CA 91604
(800) 2-BUY-YARN   (818) 766-1515

Patternworks
36A South Gate Dr.
Poughkeepsie, NY 12601
(800) 438-5464   (914) 462-8000

Personal Threads
8025 W. Dodge Rd.
Omaha, NE 68114
(800) 306-7733   (402) 391-7288
fax: (402) 391-0039
e-mail: personlt@radiks.net
www.personalthreads.com

Three Kittens Yarn Shoppe
805 Sibley Memorial Hwy.
St. Paul, MN 55118
(800) 489-4969   (612) 457-4969

Wool Connection
34 E. Main St.
Old Avon Village N.
Avon, CT 06001
(800) 933-9665   (860) 678-1710
www.woolconnection.com

Wooly Knits
6728 Lowell Ave.
McLean, VA 22101
(800) 767-4036   (703) 448-9665
www.woolyknits.com

Yarns International
5110 Ridgefield Rd., Suite 200
Bethesda, MD 20816
(800) 927-6728   (301) 913-2980

MISCELLANEOUS
Fur Luxe is distributed by:

Lane Borgosesia
P.O. Box 217
Colorado Springs, CO 80903

Dritz Fray Check is available at most
sewing and craft shops or from
the following companies:

Nancy's Notions
333 Beichl Ave.
P.O. Box 683
Beaver Dam, WI 53916
(414) 887-7321

Skeins
11309 Hwy. 7
Minnetonka, MN 55305
(612) 939-4166

Other Needlework Books from Taunton

Look for these Taunton Press books at your local bookstore or knitting retailer:

50 Heirloom Buttons to Make

Alice Starmore's Book of Fair Isle Knitting

American Country Needlepoint

Colorful Knitwear Design

Designing Knitwear

Great Knits

Hand-Knitting Techniques

Hand-Manipulated Stitches for Machine Knitters

The Jean Moss Book of World Knits

The Knit Hat Book

Knitted Sweater Style

Knitting Around the World

Knitting Counterpanes

Knitting Lace

Knitting Tips & Trade Secrets

For a catalog of Taunton's sewing and needlework books and videos, write (or call):
The Taunton Press, P.O. Box 5506, Newtown, CT 06470-5506; (800) 888-8286.